17E

ECONOMICS:
It's Your Business

by Henry Billings

The Peoples Publishing Group, Inc.

Free to Learn, to Grow, to Change

Credits

Design by Margarita T. Giammanco
Desktop Publishing Assistance and Graphics by DS Design & Printing
Copy Editing by Salvatore Allocco
Photo Research by Judith M. Kerns
Cover Design by Westchester Graphic Group
Logo Design by Wendy E. Kury
Electronic Publishing Consultant: James Fee Langendoen

Photo Credits

p. 1, Peter Gridley/FPG; p. 2, R. Maiman/Sygma; p. 3, E. Castle/Folio Inc.; p. 4, AP/Wideworld; p. 7, J. Riley/Folio, Inc.; p. 11, C. Davidson/Folio, Inc.; p. 15, E. Poggenpohl/Folio, Inc.; p. 19, J. Zaruba/Folio, Inc.; p. 22, M. Kozlowski/FPG; p. 23, T. McBride/Folio, Inc.; p. 24, UPI/Bettmann; p. 26, Courtesy of the International Ladies Garment Workers Union; p. 31, AP/Wideworld; p. 36 UPI/Bettmann; p. 38, S. Brown/Folio, Inc.; p. 39, AP/Wideworld; p. 40, D. Hallinan/FPG; p. 41, E. Poggenpohl/Folio, Inc.; p. 42, AP/Wideworld; p. 43, E. Johnson/Folio, Inc.; p. 49, J.P. Laffont/Sygma; p. 53, F. Klogman/Folio, Inc.; p. 58, Culver Pictures, Inc.; p. 67, AP/Wideworld; p. 68, A. Tannnenbaum/Sygma; p. 71, AP/Wideworld; p. 74, Koslowski/FPG; p. 78, UPI/Bettmann; p. 81, L. Freed/Magnum; p. 82, UPI/Bettmann; p. 87, UPI/Bettmann; p. 88, UPI/Bettmann; p. 98, Courtesy of the U.S.D.A.; p. 103, Van Bucher/Photo Researchers; p. 106, Courtesy of the U.S. Navy; p. 108, R. Maiman/Sygma; p. 112, Culver Pictures, Inc.; p. 114, B. Barbey/Magnum; p. 117, C. Michael Keller/FPG; p. 122, UPI/Bettmann.

Cover currency from left to right:

Canada, Netherlands, Egypt, Greece, Philippines, Russia, England, Colombia, France, India, Mexico, Mexico, Bahamas, Panama, Portugal, Italy, Russia, Israel, Jamaica, Yugoslavia, Italy, England, Norway, England, Germany, Equador, Brazil, England, Egypt, Egypt, Germany, Mexico, Netherlands, USA, Russia, Japan, Germany, USA, Libya, Mexico, Uruguay, Czechoslovakia, Colombia, Mexico, Japan.

Back cover currency from left to right:

USA, Mexico, England, Germany, Canada, USA, Belgium, Colombia, Mexico, Mexico, England, Egypt, USA, England, Norway, Canada, Jamaica, Norway, England, USA.

ISBN 1-56256-047-6
ISBN 1-56256-047-6

16 17 18 19 20

230 West Passaic Street
Maywood, New Jersey 07607

Printed in the United States of America.

Table of Contents

1

What Is Economics?

How can you become a smart consumer?

Empower Yourself - Cooperative Learning

Learning how to be a smart shopper is important. Form a group of three or five people. Choose one product that all of you might be interested in buying. It can be a computer, a CD player, a color TV—whatever you agree it will be.

Each person in the group will go to a different store that sells the product you have decided to research. Ask the price of all the models of the product that are sold at that store. Ask what features each model has. Find out what each feature does. List the price and features of each model you see.

When you have completed your research, make a chart. Across the top of the chart, write the names of the stores that everyone visited. On the left, write the brand names and models that you saw in each store. Under the name of each store, write the prices and features of the items on the left side of the chart. Leave out any models that were sold in only one store.

Discuss each model. Decide what features are worth paying more for. Circle the model that is the "best buy" and the name of the store that sells it for the lowest price.

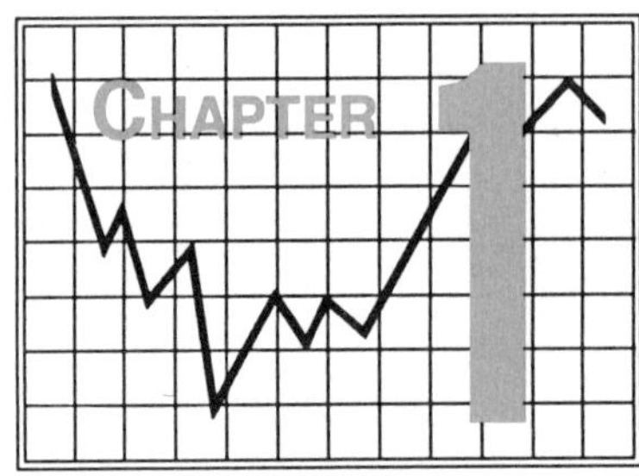

Economics and Scarcity

On Your Way Up
Preview
Before you read this unit, preview each chapter to find out what it will be about. Look for words in **bold** print in the paragraphs and in the margins. Read the questions that begin paragraphs and end each chapter. Look at the photos and illustrations. Read the captions. Predict what you will learn about in each chapter.

People and businesses have to decide what they want or need most. Governments make the same decisions. What should they spend their money on? Individuals, businesses and governments all want to make the best use of what they have. That is heart of economics.

Economics (ek-uh-NAH-miks) is a science that studies how and why goods are produced and used. Economics is also the study of making choices. People must choose what to buy, when to buy, from whom to buy and how much to pay. All people are faced with the problem of how to spend their money. No one is so rich or powerful that he or she can have everything.

economics
a science that studies how and why goods are produced and used

Economics is a study of the choices people must make about what to buy, when to buy and from whom to buy.

Why study economics? The study of economics helps you to understand the power of money in your hands as well as in the hands of others. Understanding economics helps you to make better choices when you spend your money. Knowing about economics helps you to think more clearly about career decisions you must make. Economics also helps to make you a better citizen. As a voter, you can voice your opinion on how the government raises and spends money.

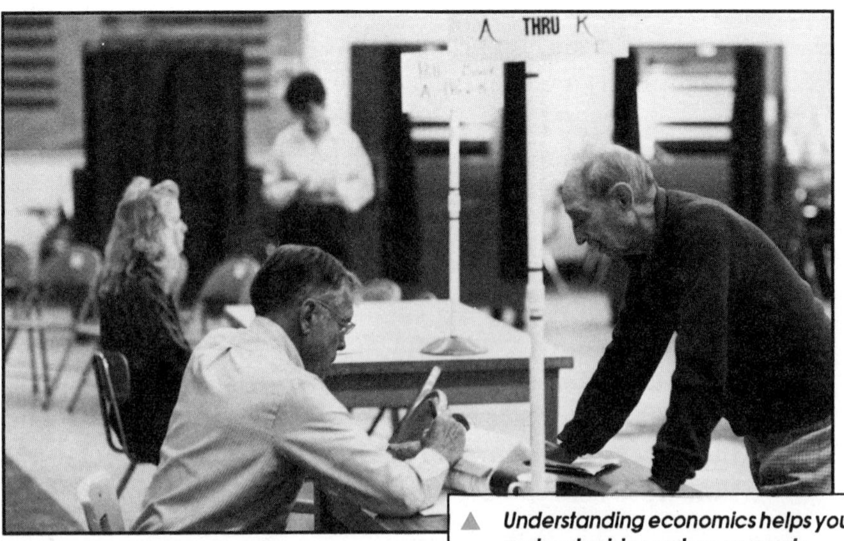

Understanding economics helps you make decisions when you vote.

What is scarcity? The first law of economics will not allow anyone to "have it all." Economists call this law **scarcity** (SKAIR-suh-tee). Scarcity means that there are limited supplies of everything. "There's only so much to go around." How many times have you heard that? According to economics, there really is only so much to go around. No one can have everything he or she wants. This applies to you as an individual. It applies to businesses. It applies to governments as well.

scarcity
a condition of limited resources

If people were willing to settle for whatever they got, there would be no problem. In fact, there would be no economics. Of course, no one is so easily satisfied. People want much more than they have. People do not all start in the same place, either. The wants and needs of people with low incomes can be very different from those with high incomes.

What can you do about scarcity? You must make **trade-offs**, or choices. A trade-off is the act of choosing which things you want most. This is the second law of economics. If you decide to buy one thing, that money cannot buy something else. The dollars you spend on new sneakers cannot be spent on movie tickets or a sweatshirt. The money a business spends on a new computer cannot be spent on a truck. The money the government spends on defense cannot be spent on health care or education.

trade-off
the act of choosing which things are most wanted

What are opportunity costs? Not only can you not have everything, but you can't do everything. Your **resources** (REE-sors-ez), the things you have to fill your needs, are limited. When you buy something, you are using the resource called money. You must choose how and when to use the money you have. Once again, resources are not the same for everyone. People with fewer resources have fewer choices. What you lose when you choose to do one thing rather than another is called an **opportunity cost** (op-ur-TOO-nuh-tee).

resources
the supply of things that people have to fill their needs

opportunity cost
whatever a person cannot have because he or she has spent resources on something else

When you use your resources to buy clothing, you cannot spend the same resources on other things.

Critical Thinking
What opportunity costs do you have when you spend your money?

Businesses have to make choices, too. Time spent planning new products cannot be spent training new sales people. Even the United States government has its opportunity costs. Steel used to build tanks cannot be used to build bridges or aircraft carriers.

What do economists do? Economics is the study of making choices. Scarcity forces everyone to make choices. Economists try to solve problems caused by scarcity. They do this by studying how scarcity affects people, companies and governments.

Economists study the ways in which individuals, businesses and governments use their resources.

Suppose the XYZ Company hired an economist. The economist would look at the way XYZ uses its resources. The economist would then suggest better ways to use those resources. In other words, the economist would try to give the company better ways to deal with scarcity.

William H. Gray III, Chairman of the House Budget Committee, makes economic decisions with Congress.

Economists also try to tell what will happen in the future. This is not an easy task. Economics is not an exact science, like biology and chemistry. Sometimes one concept or principle will clash with another. An economic rule that works for one company might not work for another. For this reason, economists often disagree with each other.

Economics is not an exact science. Economists often disagree.

Economists have their own values and ideas about how to do things. Two economists looking at the same problem might come up with totally different answers.

What is microeconomics? Economists have two ways to study an economy. One is called **microeconomics** (MY-kroh-ek-uh-NAHM-iks). Microeconomics is like a microscope. A microeconomist studies the small details of the economy. For example, a microeconomist might look at how one company makes its choices. What resources does the company use? What prices does it charge for its products? How is it meeting the challenges of other companies?

microeconomics
the study of the small details of an economy

Microeconomics also looks at choices made by individuals. What products do they buy? What prices are they willing to pay? What are the opportunity costs for certain choices?

What is macroeconomics? The other way to study an economy is **macroeconomics** (MAK-roh-ek-uh-NAHM-iks). Macroeconomics, like a telescope, looks at the big picture. Macroeconomics looks at the economy as a whole.

macroeconomics
the study of an economy as a whole

Macroeconomists study such topics as the total amount of money in use. They look at how many people have jobs as well as how many people are out of work. Macroeconomists look at how much the nation produces and what is happening to the value of money. They also want to know whether the nation's economy is growing—and how fast.

Understanding What You Read

1. What is economics?
2. Explain the law of scarcity.
3. Why do economists sometimes disagree with each other?
4. How does scarcity affect the government?
5. What is the difference between microeconomics and macroeconomics?

Workbook Activities

Chapter Test, p. 2
Decision Making, p. 3

Money Matters

One of the basic questions in economics is "who gets what?" For the most part, the answer to that question is "the person with money." The new sports car goes to the person who has the $40,000 to spend. A hot new CD goes to whoever can afford the price tag.

Money is anything that people will accept as payment for something they are selling.

What is money? Money can be anything. It can be clam shells, beaver skins, rice or glass beads. The important thing is whether people will accept it as payment for something they are selling. Suppose the government of the United States said that walnuts could be used as money. Walnuts could be used to pay taxes, buy food and pay bills. Suppose that everyone agreed with this new arrangement. Walnuts would become money. Money is, therefore, anything that people will accept as money.

Why is money necessary? In a world without money, it would be hard to buy and sell things. Without money, you would have to trade things for other things. If you had a chicken to sell and you wanted to buy corn, you would exchange the chicken for the corn. Of course, you would have to find someone with corn who also wants your chicken.

barter
to exchange one thing of value for another thing of value

What is this system called? This system of trade is called **barter** (BART-ur). Barter can work. However, it can only work in a certain kinds of societies. These societies are usually based on agriculture. Barter would not work well in a modern society with advanced technology. Such societies are too complicated.

Just think what it would be like to have a barter system in the United States today. How many bushels of corn would be worth a year of schooling? Would the salesperson in the shopping mall take your chicken in exchange for a wall poster? How many haircuts would be worth a flight from Boston, Massachusetts, to Atlanta, Georgia?

Clearly, a barter system would make everyday life in the United States very difficult. For barter to work, you must have what the other person needs, and the other person must have what you need. The barter system is a very awkward way of getting the things you want or need. This problem can be solved through the use of money.

What is a medium of exchange? Money is a **medium of exchange** (MEE-dee-um of eks-CHAYNJ). A medium of exchange is something of value that will pay for the things you want. Money can be used to buy what people want. Since everyone agrees that money has worth, everyone is willing to accept it in exchange.

medium of exchange anything that everyone accepts as payment for products or services

Why is money helpful? Since the medium of exchange is money, most things can be measured in it. In the United States, the value of things is measured in dollars. Other countries have different names for their money. In France, for example, the main unit of money is called the franc (FRANK). In Mexico the value of things is measured by the peso (PAY-soh) . In India the rupee (ROO-pee) is the main unit of money, and in Malawi it is the kwacha (KWAH-chah).

A complex economy needs a medium of exchange—money—that has a set value that everyone agrees to.

How many haircuts will pay for an airline ticket?

The use of money makes it easy to set values for things. By measuring haircuts and airplane flights in American dollars, you know how many haircuts are worth a flight from Boston to Atlanta. A haircut has a price. So does an airline ticket. A certain number of haircuts equals one plane ticket. In this way, money measures the value of whatever you might want to buy.

Money can also be set aside and saved. In an economy using barter, it is difficult to save anything. How would you save chickens until you had enough to make a down payment on a car? There is no way to put such things in a bank.

Money has to do three things. First, money has to last. The ink cannot run if the money gets wet. Money cannot easily rot or crumble. Second, money should be light enough to carry in your pocket or purse. This is a major advantage of paper money. Third, money should come in many different values, such as nickels, dimes, quarters and dollar bills.

Money must last, be light enough to carry and come in many different values.

What kinds of money are there? Coins and paper money, sometimes called **currency** (KUR-en-see), are what most people think of when they think of money. However, coins and paper money make up less than one-fourth of the money supply. The rest comes from checks.

currency
a term used to describe a medium of exchange in circulation, such as money

The money that people have in their checking accounts is called **demand deposits**. People can demand their deposits back simply by writing checks. People can write checks up to the amount of money they have on deposit at the bank.

demand deposits
money kept in a checking account that a person can get back, or demand, by writing a check or making a withdrawal

Most people and businesses pay their bills by check. In fact, more than 90 percent of all the money exchanged in the United States today is exchanged by check. People pay by check because it is easy, and it is safer than carrying cash. Checks are so widely used today that they are considered a form of money. Figure 1 shows the amount of demand deposits in the money supply.

More than 90 percent of all the money exchanged in the United States is exchanged by check.

Reading a Bar Graph
Bar graphs usually show a series of two or more bars along the horizontal axis, the line across the bottom. The vertical axis, the line on the left side, shows the value of the bars. A key located either below the graph or to the side tells what the bars stand for.

Figure 1

Demand Deposits in the Money Supply

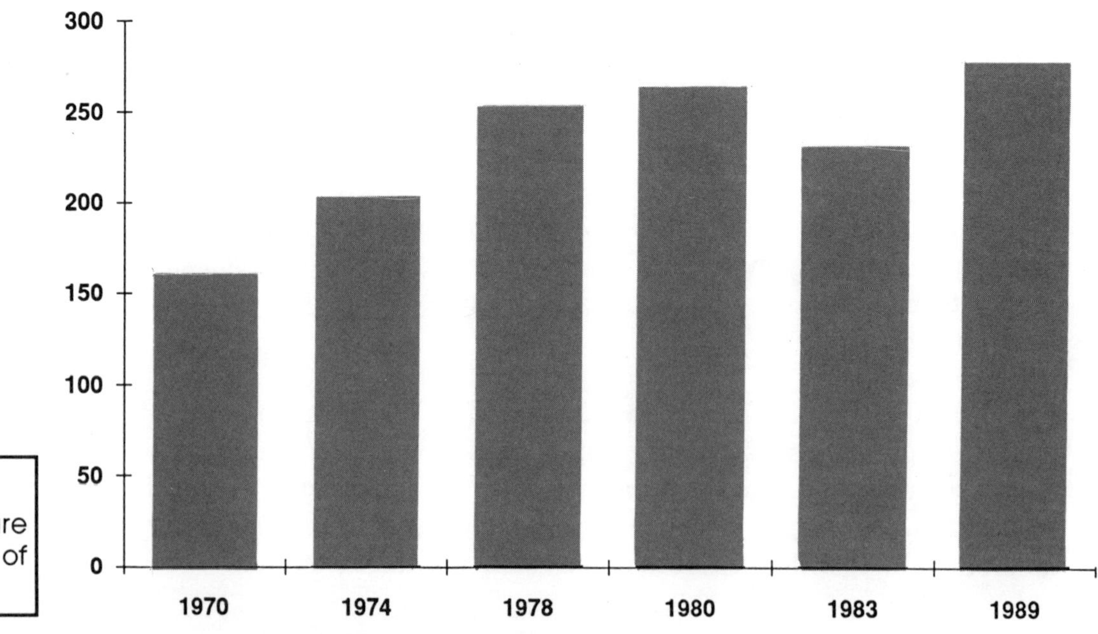

Adapted from *Statistical Abstract*, 1990.

People who want to buy things are not limited to only currency and checks. Many people now buy things on **credit**. They buy things today that they pay for later. Most people use credit cards. All they have to do is to sign their names on a charge slip. They can then pay their bills sometime in the future. Credit cards can be thought of as a kind of money. Some people even think that credit cards will one day replace currency and checks as a way of doing business.

credit
the ability to buy something with a promise to pay later

Does the value of money change? Diamonds and gold nuggets are valuable because they are scarce. The same rule applies to money. Dollar bills have value because there are only so many of them. If money grew on trees, it would be worthless. After all, money is just paper. Even diamonds or gold nuggets would lose most of their value if they were common stones that could be found in any park or backyard. To have value, any medium of exchange must be fairly scarce.

Critical Thinking
Could diamonds or gold nuggets be a medium of exchange? Why or why not?

Suppose the United States government suddenly decided to double the amount of money in use. Suppose everyone received twice as much money as they had before, and everyone's wages were also doubled. Would anyone really be richer as a result? No! If everyone's wages were doubled, then the price of the products they make would have to cost twice as much. In other words, you would have the same amount of things being bought with twice as much money. The amount of money does not matter. The amount of money compared to the amount of things available is important.

The value of money depends on the amount of money in circulation compared to the amount of things that can be bought.

The supply of money must be controlled. For the most part, the government controls the supply of money. Taxing and spending are two ways in which the government affects the money supply.

On Your Way Up
Review
After you finish reading this chapter, write a summary about the different kinds of money. Write your summary in your own words so you will remember it.

Understanding What You Read

1. What is the barter system?
2. What is a medium of exchange?
3. What are demand deposits?
4. What is credit?
5. Why are checks considered to be a form of money?

Workbook Activities

Chapter Test, p. 4
Making a Bar Graph, p. 5

The Role of the Consumer - Part 1

consumer
a person who uses a product or a service

free market
condition in which buying and selling take place

In the American economy, you—the **consumer** (kun-SOO-mur)—are the star. The consumer helps to decide what will be produced. The consumer can make or break a company. The money spent by the consumer sends the whole economy up or down. The consumer controls the economy by "voting." The consumer does not vote in a polling booth. The voting is done in the **free market**, where buying and selling take place.

The consumer controls the economy by spending — or not spending — money.

How does the consumer "vote"? Think of each consumer dollar as a "vote." The consumer votes for all kinds of things he or she wants. What will the consumer vote for? That depends on the choice of each consumer. Every dollar spent for a hamburger at Harry's Hamburger Heaven is a vote for Harry's Hamburger Heaven. It is also a vote not given to any other fast-food restaurant. If a business gets many consumer votes, it will probably make money and be a success. If it gets very few votes, it will be out of business.

There is another difference between consumer voting and voting in a polling booth. When you vote in an election, every voter has just one vote. That is the democratic way. Consumer voting doesn't work that way. The more money you have to spend, the more consumer votes you have. Someone who spends $100,000 a year will have more impact on the economy than someone who spends $10,000. That may or may not be fair, but that is the way the economy works.

Everyone is a consumer.

Who is the consumer? Few questions are this easy to answer. You are a consumer—and so is everyone else. You do not have to buy something to be a consumer. You just have to use it. Anyone who rides on a subway or drinks a cup of tea or goes to the movies is a consumer. That makes everyone a consumer.

Critical Thinking
Can an animal be a consumer? Explain.

People spend their whole lives as consumers. Infants may not buy diapers, but they surely use them. Someone who has just died may be a consumer as well. In most cases, the person will need a casket, the services of a funeral home and a plot of land for burial. In short, everyone is a consumer from the cradle to the grave. It would be impossible to find someone who doesn't consume something.

Have consumers changed? Two hundred years ago, most people took care of themselves. Many city families as well as frontier families made their own clothes. They often grew their own food. If people got sick, a family member usually took care of them. Most Americans were more independent back then. They didn't need to buy as many things as people do today. The United States has become a "consumer economy." In that sense, the world has grown more and more complex.

What is today's consumer like? Today's consumer is bombarded with choices. In the early days of our nation, people would have been lucky to find two different brands of soap. Most of the time they bought whatever was available, or they made their own soap. Today, there are a hundred different kinds of soap. There is a soap that promises to make you look young. One soap is supposed to have "sex appeal." Another soap claims that it is for "the real man."

The American economy gives consumers many choices.

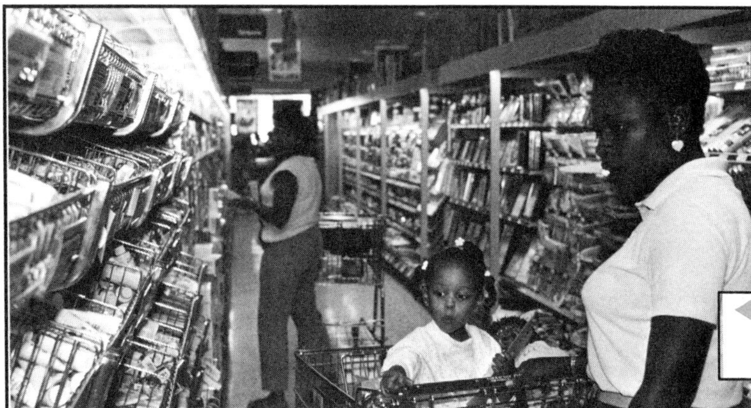

Consumers in the United States have many choices.

Do all consumers have choices? Most American consumers today are faced with almost endless choices. Even underwear comes in a rainbow of colors. Every year, car models change. It is very hard to know what to buy. One company claims one thing. Another company claims something else. You, the consumer, are in the middle of all this. With your dollar vote, you are in control. Unfortunately, you have so many choices to make that it is easy to become confused.

On Your Way Up
Fact and Opinion
A fact states something that can be proved. An opinion is a belief. You say that the brand of sneakers you wear is the best on the market. Is this a fact or an opinion?

Most Americans are flooded with choices—but not all Americans. Choice for low-income people is not the same as it is for high-income people. Some people may be able to buy only the lowest-priced soap or breakfast cereal or bread. For more costly items, such as a new car, they might not have any choice at all.

The number of choices a consumer has depends on the consumer's income.

Are all consumers alike? Everyone is a consumer, but no two consumers are exactly alike. All people have their own personal needs and wants. They have their own likes and dislikes. Most people cannot buy everything they want. Their incomes are just too small. People have to make some tough choices. If they buy new clothes for school, they might not be able to buy a new sofa for the living room. One new winter coat might mean that the CD player must last another year.

> **Reading a Circle Graph**
> The circle graph, or pie chart, shows the parts of a whole. The circle represents the whole, or 100 percent. It is then divided into parts.

How Personal Income Is Spent

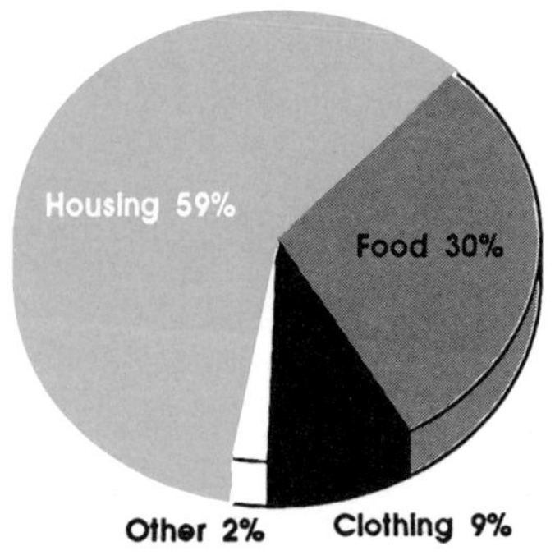

Figure 1. Income: $5,000- $10,000

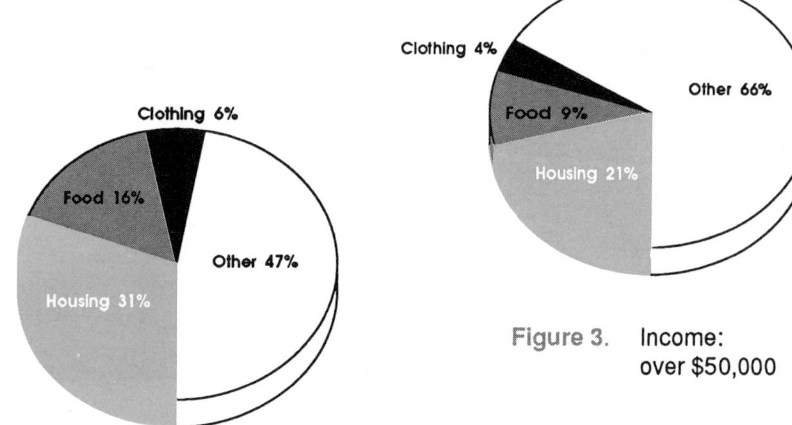

Figure 3. Income: over $50,000

Figure 2. Income: $20,000- $30,000

How do people spend their money? Look at Figures 1, 2 and 3. Figure 1 shows the percentage of total income spent on food, housing and clothing by families who earn between $5,000 and $10,000 a year. Figure 2 shows the percentage of total income spent on the same items by families earning between $20,000 and $30,000 a year. Figure 3 shows the percentages for families earning over $50,000 a year. These figures do not change much from year to year.

> **Critical Thinking**
> Why do families earning over $50,000 a year spend only 9 percent of their income on food?

Food, housing and clothing are, of course, basic needs for all people. These circle graphs show that high-income people do not spend their money the same way as low-income people. Look at the share of income spent on food. Families that earn between $5,000 and $10,000 spend 30 percent of their income just on food. On the other hand, families that earn between $20,000 and $30,000 spend only 16 percent to eat. Families with incomes over $50,000 spend just 9 percent of their income on food.

Does the same rule apply to housing and clothing? Lower-income families have to spend 59 percent of their income to put a roof over their heads. The middle-income families spend 31 percent on housing. The high-income families spend just 21 percent on housing.

High-income families are much more likely to own their own homes. Low-income families are much more likely to rent. Families earning between $5,000 and $10,000 spend 19 percent on rent. Families earning more than $50,000 spend, on average, about 1 percent!

The lowest-income families spend 9 percent on clothing. The middle families spend 6 percent and the high-income families spend just 4 percent.

Critical Thinking

If a family's income suddenly doubled, would the family spend a larger or smaller percentage of its income on clothing? Explain.

Remember that these numbers represent a share, or percentage, of income. In terms of straight dollars, the high-income families spend more on food, housing and clothing than the low-income families. For example, in 1989 families with more than $50,000 in income spent about $7,000 a year on food. Families who earned between $5,000 and $10,000 spent about $2,300 on food.

How does income affect spending? Families with the lowest incomes must spend almost all their money just to survive. They have to spend a total of 98 percent (30+59+9) on their basic needs! Those families earning more than $50,000 must spend just 34 percent (9+21+4) on the same needs.

As income increases, the percentage of income spent on basic needs decreases.

The higher a family's income, the more money they have left to spend on other things. They can spend more on travel. They have the money to go to Europe. They are also more likely to have money for such things as private schooling and tennis lessons.

People have different amounts of money and they spend their money in different ways. However, they do spend money. As a result, the United States has a great consumer economy. Each year, American consumers spend trillions of dollars. There are two other large consumers. They are business and government. Together, they make up the other third of all spending.

Understanding What You Read

1. How do consumers vote?
2. In what ways are consumers today different from consumers 200 years ago?
3. Are some consumers more important to the economy than others? Explain.

Workbook Activities

Chapter Test, p. 6
Reading a Circle Graph, p. 7

The Role of the Consumer - Part 2

The consumer can be very powerful. Much of this power comes from the wide range of choices the consumer has. With almost every purchase, the consumer has a choice. No one is forced to buy from just one company.

competition
the effort of two or more sellers to attract the business of a buyer by offering the most favorable terms

Think about supermarkets. In most places, supermarkets try to price items so that shoppers will come to their stores instead of to others. This is called **competition** (kom-puh-TISH-un). Supermarkets run full-page advertisements in newspapers because they are competing with other supermarkets. Each store must let consumers know what the special prices are for the week. No supermarket can stay in business if its prices are too high for people to pay.

Critical Thinking
Besides having weekly specials, what else can food stores do to compete?

Can the consumer say no? The consumer has the last word. What if the consumer decides not to buy? When the consumer decides not to buy from a store, the store goes out of business. Each year thousands of businesses close their doors. For one reason or another, the consumer said no.

What happens when the consumer says no to a whole industry? The impact is powerful. Thousands of workers lose their jobs and many businesses fail. Look at what happened to the auto industry. During the 1970s and 1980s, many consumers said no to the large American car. They switched to smaller Japanese cars, which they felt were better built. Many American workers lost their jobs. Plants closed. One major auto maker almost went out of business.

boycott
a refusal to buy a product or a service

What is a boycott? During the 1970s beef prices were going up fast. Suddenly, consumers decided to stop buying beef. This is called a **boycott** (BOI-kot). Large numbers of consumers simply decided not to buy any more beef. They ate chicken or fish instead. For one week, millions of Americans refused to buy or eat beef. Ranchers were thrown into a panic. What were they going to do with their cattle? Warehouses and food stores suddenly had more beef than they could sell. The boycott lasted only a week. The consumer won. Beef prices came down, and people soon went back to their old eating habits. But the boycott clearly showed the power of the consumer.

Consumers can boycott, or refuse to buy, products. Boycotts show the power of the consumer.

Consumers boycotted beef until the price went down.

There was a more recent example. In the late 1980s, many people stopped buying tuna fish. The reason was not because the selling price was too high. The consumers were angry because tuna boats were catching and killing dolphins in their nets. Slowly, this boycott forced the fishing industry to change its ways. Fishing boats started to use different nets that allowed dolphins to escape. Some tuna fish canners began to put a notice on their labels that said that no dolphins had been harmed. Again, the consumers won the day.

On Your Way Up
Cause and Effect
A *cause* brings about a change in something. The change is called the *effect*. What caused the consumers to boycott tuna fish? What was the effect of the boycott?

Who protects the consumer? Consumers as a group can be all-powerful. However, sometimes they need protection from people who have products to sell. Competition can be fierce. Every seller is looking for an edge. Some sellers go too far. They try to cheat the consumer. In such cases, the consumer needs protection. For this reason, there are laws and agencies to help consumers.

Laws and government agencies help to protect the consumer from dishonest sellers.

No one can protect the consumer from everything. There are some things the consumer should know. Price is one of them. If you always buy apples where they cost the most, who is to blame? It is easy enough to compare prices. You should know the limits of your income. How much money must you have for your basic needs? How much should you have in the bank in case of an emergency? Answering such questions will help you to plan your spending. But there are some times when even the smartest consumers need help.

What is a monopoly? The consumer has to be protected from **monopoly** (muh-NOP-uh-lee). A monopoly occurs when one company completely controls a market. The United States has laws that prevent this from happening. A monopoly can result in prices that are too high and products that are low in quality. The consumer is not powerful enough to deal with monopolies. The government takes legal action to prevent them.

monopoly
the complete ownership of a market by one seller

Laws protect the consumer from false advertising.

What is false advertising? The government also protects the consumer from false advertising. At times, companies will make wild claims. The consumer has no way to check out the truth of these claims in most cases. False claims were once made about brands of aspirin. Aspirin is aspirin. One aspirin tablet is as good as another. For a long time most people did not know that. Many drug companies claimed that their aspirin was better than anyone else's. Most consumers are not chemists. They could not check out these claims in a lab.

Laws protect the consumer from harmful products.

Can products be harmful? Some products are dangerous, and consumers need to be protected from them. Again, most consumers are not able to perform laboratory tests on the products they buy. Who will protect the consumer from a face cream that causes a rash? What about children's clothes that can easily catch fire? In such cases, consumers need the help of an expert. They need someone to point out or possibly ban products that can hurt them.

Labels must tell consumers what is in food products.

What must labels show? Most food products have their contents clearly labeled. Does your ice cream really contain cream? Some do not! They contain something called "nonfat milk solids." What chemicals were used to make your brownie mix? What really went into the making of your favorite hot dog?

Labels on processed food products must tell you what the ingredients are, that is, what is in them. All the ingredients are listed on the label. The first ingredient listed is the most common one. The second ingredient is the second most common one, and so on. Such labels are required by law.

INGREDIENTS: WHOLE WHEAT FLOUR, ENRICHED WHEAT FLOUR (CONTAINS NIACIN, IRON, THIAMINE, VITAMIN B, CALCIUM, VITAMIN C), SUGAR, SALT, PEPPER, RIBOFLAVIN, VEGETABLE SHORTENING (SOYBEAN OIL), EGG WHITE, HIGH FRUCTOSE CORN SYRUP, MALTED BARLEY FLOUR, ARTIFICIAL COLORS.

▲ *Food labels must tell you what is in the product.*

What are interest rates? A bank that lends you money must tell you exactly how much you will have to pay in interest rates. Interest (IN-tur-ist) is the amount charged for taking out a loan. There can be no hidden service fees. You must be told that a 1 1/2 percent monthly interest rate equals an 18 percent yearly interest rate. The total cost of the loan must be clearly spelled out. The final cost must be given in dollars. Then anyone can know the true cost.

Critical Thinking
Why do you have to pay interest when you borrow money?

Where can a consumer go for help? As a consumer, you have certain rights. The government works to protect you. The local board of health, for example, will regularly inspect your neighborhood restaurants. The board of health wants to see if the food is being properly stored and if the kitchen is clean. The Federal Trade Commission is supposed to watch out for misleading or false advertising. The Food and Drug Administration tries to protect us from harmful foods and drugs.

Government agencies such as the Federal Trade Commission and the Food and Drug Administration protect the consumer.

Private agencies, such as the Better Business Bureau, try to stop unfair treatment of consumers. If you have a problem, check your telephone book. Government agencies and private agencies will be listed. If you don't know which agency to contact, call your city hall and ask for help. In addition, the federal government prints more than 200 consumer booklets. You can get them by writing to the Consumer Information Center, Pueblo, Colorado 81009.

Understanding What You Read

1. What can consumers do if they do not like a product?
2. What is false advertising?
3. Which government and private agencies protect consumers?
4. Why is it important to know what the interest rate is when you are taking out a loan?

Workbook Activities

Chapter Test, p. 8
Reading a Comparing Product Labels, p. 9

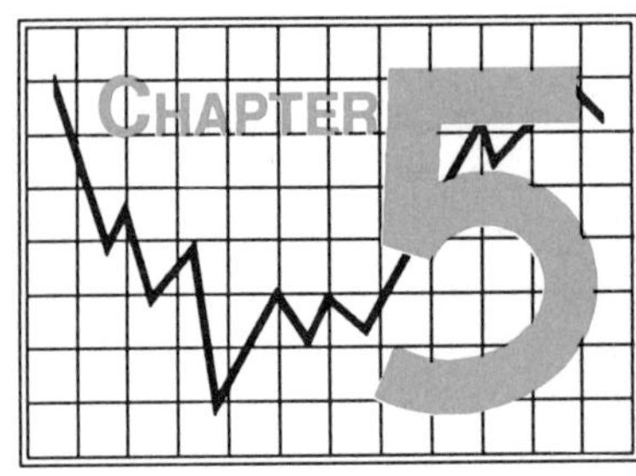

The Role of the Producer

All four factors of production are needed to make the products that consumers buy.

The basic question in economics is: How do people produce what they want? How, for example, do people produce a loaf of bread or a pint of ice cream? To answer these questions, it is necessary to know the **f**actors of production (FAK-torz of pruh-DUK-shun). The factors of production are used to produce goods and services. The four basic factors of production are land, labor, capital and management.

What does land provide? Perhaps it is easier to think of land in terms of a nation's natural resources. Land includes everything above, on or under the soil. Gold, diamonds and oil are natural resources. Fertile fields and forests are, too. Lakes and rivers and even the air you breathe are natural resources.

Land provides both renewable and nonrenewable resources.

What are renewable and nonrenewable resources? Some natural resources are renewable (rih-NOO-uh-bul). These resources can be replaced as they are being used. The forests are a good example. People can cut down trees and then plant new ones. Most natural resources, however, are nonrenewable (non-rih-NOO-uh-bul). These resources cannot be replaced. Once they are used, they are gone forever. Oil and coal are examples of natural resources that are not renewable.

Critical Thinking

Is building a shopping mall on a riverbank a good or a bad use of land? Why?

What affects land use? Since land is a limited resource, it must be used in the best way possible. Land used for one purpose cannot be used for something else. For instance, the flat land along the banks of rivers is the best farming land. The spring floods bring minerals that enrich the soil. This flat land is also ideal for building shopping malls and homes. As a result, the United States is losing some of its best farm land every year.

What is labor? The people who make products are labor (LAY-bur). By providing labor, humans create wealth. Labor means the skills and talents of people. Like natural resources, not all human resources are the same. One group of one hundred people might produce ten times as much as another group of one hundred people.

productivity
a measure of how effectively workers are working

What makes the difference? There are three reasons why one group of workers may perform better than another. First, there is **productivity** (proh-duk-TIV-ih-tee). Healthy people are able to work better than sick people. If workers receive good health care and eat good food, they will be more productive.

Then there is the matter of skill. Skill is the ability to do a task. Highly skilled people produce more than unskilled people. Highly skilled people are trained to make better use of their tools. Skilled carpenters, bricklayers and plumbers can build more and better houses than unskilled workers. At one time, almost all labor was unskilled. Now machines do the work of most unskilled labor.

Once almost all labor was unskilled. Now machines do the work of most unskilled labor.

Most jobs today require skilled workers.

Motivation (moh-tih-VAY-shun) has an important effect on productivity. In some companies, when production goes up, so does the paycheck. Money is powerful motivation.

motivation
an extra benefit, such as a bonus, that gets workers to produce more

What is capital? Most people think of **capital** (KAP-ih-tul) as money, and it is. However, in economic terms, capital is much more than money. Capital is the total of all buildings, tools and factories. Capital is also the total of highways, pipelines, trucks and ships.

capital
physical items, such as money or goods, that help workers produce wealth

The physical items that help workers produce wealth are called capital goods (KAP-ih-tul GOODZ). Land and labor are used to make what are called capital goods. These capital goods, such as factory buildings and machines, are used to make either more capital goods or things for the consumer.

What is the role of management? The last factor of production is **management** (MAN-ij-ment), the people who make the decisions. In some ways, management may be thought of as part of labor. After all, management is a human resource. However, in a modern economy the managers have a separate role. Labor actually makes the product, but managers decide how. They are the ones who decide how to mix land, labor and capital.

management
people who combine land, labor and capital to produce goods and services

Management uses land, labor and capital to produce goods and services.

What are goods and services? What do the four factors of production produce? Economists use the term *goods and services*. Goods and services are things that humans want and need. Goods are physical objects produced for a consumer. A toaster is a good. A car, a button, a pizza and a magazine are also goods.

Services are work done for the benefit of consumers. Services cannot be seen or touched. A teacher provides a service. So do lawyers, doctors and social workers. When you ride on a bus, what are you paying for? You are not buying the bus. You are buying a service. The bus company is providing you with a service.

durable goods
goods that can be used over and over

nondurable goods
goods that can be used only a few times

What are durable and nondurable goods? Goods can be looked at in several different ways. There are **durable goods** (DOO-ruh-bul GOODZ) and **nondurable goods** (NON-DOO-ruh-bul GOODZ). Durable goods last a long time. They can be used over and over again. An oven is an good example of a durable good. Nondurable goods, on the other hand, do not last long. A fresh peach is a nondurable good. So are a piece of chalk and a gallon of gasoline.

On Your Way Up
Reread
Read the paragraphs that discuss the factors of production. Make a list of the factors of production. Write a description of each factor in your own words.

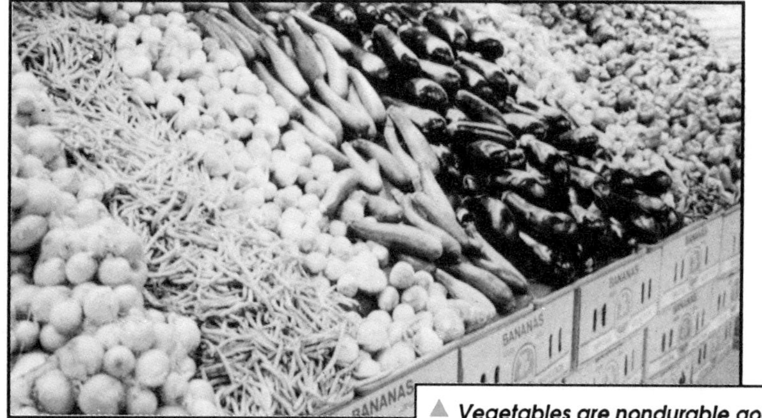

▲ *Vegetables are nondurable goods.*

consumer goods
products made for use by people

producer goods
products used to make consumer goods or services

What are consumer and producer goods? A consumer is someone who uses a good or service for personal use. A **consumer good** (kun-SOO-mur GOOD) is any good made for personal use. A basketball is a consumer good. A producer is someone who makes a good or provides a service for someone else. A **producer good** (pruh-DOO-sur GOOD) is used to make money. A producer good helps the producer to make a living. It is used to produce other goods and services.

The difference between a consumer good and a producer good is how that good is used. A car is a consumer good, but a taxi cab is a producer good. It is used to provide a service to passengers. An oven in a private home is a consumer good, but an oven in a restaurant is a producer good.

What are necessities and luxuries? Goods can also be classified as necessities or luxuries. People want many things, but what do they really need? Necessities (nuh-SES-uh-teez) are the things that people must have in order to survive. Luxuries (LUK-shur-eez) are the things that people want but can live without. Food, shelter and clothing are necessities. However, prime ribs, mansions and mink coats are luxuries. The richer a country is, the more likely its people are to regard luxuries, such as washing machines and television sets, as necessities.

Goods can be classified as necessities or luxuries.

How does changing technology affect workers? Labor-saving tools increase a worker's ability to produce. These tools make workers more productive. Such tools can also give workers more free time. People have learned to let machines work for them. As a result, the average American works fewer hours and has more things than Americans fifty or a hundred years ago.

Labor-saving tools can be a mixed blessing. When **technology** (tek-NOL-uh-jee) changes, the workers must also change. Technology is changing rapidly. The computer is just one of many tools that have changed the workplace. Anyone who works with a computer must learn new skills every year because computers are constantly being improved. Each improvement means that people have a new skill to learn.

technology
a scientific way of producing goods and services

Today's workers cannot count on their training and skills to last a lifetime. They must be prepared to learn new ways of doing things. Sometimes, workers will lose their jobs because of technology. These workers must be trained to do different jobs. This is why an advanced economy needs educated workers. Workers who can read and write can be trained over and over again.

Understanding What You Read

1. What are the factors of production?
2. Name one renewable resource and two nonrenewable resources.
3. What three things affect labor?
4. What do managers do?
5. What is the difference between a consumer good and a producer good?

Workbook Activities

Chapter Test, p. 10
Making a Circle Graph, p. 11

Capitalism and the Free Enterprise System

capitalism
an economic system based on private ownership of property that is operated for profit

Every economic system has money, consumers and producers. Every system does not have economic freedom. The United States economic system, called **capitalism** (KAP-ih-tul-izm), is free. Capitalism is the freedom of consumers and producers to spend their money as they see fit. Freedom is what makes the American economic system work.

What were the ideas of Adam Smith? Capitalism is a fairly new idea. It has been around for only about 200 years. The idea started with a man from Scotland named Adam Smith. In 1776, Smith wrote *The Wealth of Nations*. His book changed the way people looked at themselves and at society.

Adam Smith believed that no one should control the exchange of goods and services. This idea is called capitalism.

Smith had one powerful idea. He believed in the free exchange of goods and services. No one else did. The British government closely controlled most buying and selling. For example, the government said who had the right to sell tea. Smith argued that people ought to be able to buy and sell whatever they want. He saw no place for the government in economics.

▲ *Under capitalism, anyone can sell tea.*

What is a free market? Smith said that in a free market, people look out for their own best interest. They do not think of others. The self-interest of the seller is to make money. The self-interest of the worker is to earn a high wage. The self-interest of the consumer is to get as much as possible with a given amount of money. Everyone looks out for number one. Yet Smith thought this was a great system. When everyone follows his or her self-interest, Smith said, it is good for society.

Critical Thinking Would Adam Smith have liked the law that says workers must be paid a minimum wage?

What is the "invisible hand" of the market? Why should all this self-interest be good for society? Smith said that an "invisible hand" makes the system work. The "invisible hand" is the unseen law of the market. No government is needed to set fair prices. No government is needed to ensure good quality. No government is needed to guarantee a fair wage. All these things are done by the market.

The "invisible hand" of the market is the force that creates fair prices, good products and a fair wage.

How exactly does this work? Suppose you want to buy a hamburger. Where do you go? You go to the place that offers the best hamburger for the best price. What happens to the restaurant owner who tries to charge twice as much as anyone else? If the hamburger is not truly amazing, the restaurant will probably go out of business.

As long as there are many buyers and many sellers, no one can charge an unfair price. This benefits everyone. No one can control the market. Instead, the market controls everything. According to Smith, the market's "invisible hand" forces fair prices, good products and a fair wage.

What is free enterprise? At the heart of capitalism is **free enterprise** (FREE EN-tur-pryz) . Free enterprise is the right to go into business for yourself. For example, anyone with enough money can open a flower shop. Once you have a flower shop business, you can decide how to run it. You can open your shop any hours you want, decorate it any way you want and charge whatever you want for a dozen roses.

free enterprise
the freedom of people to enter into any legal business that they wish to work in

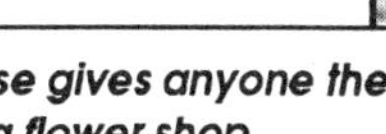

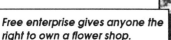

Free enterprise gives anyone the right to own a flower shop.

Free enterprise is limited by certain laws made to protect the public.

Are there limits on free enterprise? Free enterprise has some limits. Free enterprise does not mean that you can do anything. You cannot book bets on horse races or football games in most states. You cannot sell illegal drugs on a street corner. That is a crime, not free enterprise. You cannot simply declare yourself a doctor of medicine. To practice medicine, you need a license.

Competition forces businesses to produce better goods and services at low prices.

profit
money made from a business

Why is competition good? Free enterprise leads to competition. This is natural enough. If the market is open to everyone, there will always be competition. This is good for the consumer. Competition means better goods and services at low prices. Competition also keeps businesses on their toes. If they want to make money, or a **profit** (PRAHF-it), businesses have to keep the consumer happy. This drive for profit makes capitalism work.

Remember the best hamburger example. What if the only place you could get a hamburger was at Harry's Hamburger Heaven? Would Harry's run special sales? Would Harry's set up playgrounds for children? Would Harry's have strict controls over the quality of its products? Probably not! Without competition from other hamburger places, Harry's Hamburger Heaven would not have to do anything special. Consumers would have no choice. If they wanted hamburgers, they would have to go to Harry's or go without.

Under capitalism, no one can be denied the right to own property.

What rights do you have under capitalism? The right to own property is very important under capitalism. You have the right to own land. You have the right to own a car. You have the right to own a house anywhere in the country. To deny anyone these rights because of race or religion or sex is wrong. It is also against the law!

On Your Way Up
Summarize
Write a summary, or brief description, of the way in which the free enterprise system works. Write your description in your own words.

You also have the right to own a factory and hire workers. On the other hand, workers have the right to form unions and to go on strike. No one can force anyone to work for anyone else. All workers have the right to do the work of their choice. All workers also have the right to support politicians who promise to help the worker.

Capitalism gives everyone the right to own an automobile.

What is a mixed economy? The United States has a capitalist system. It is not the "pure" system that Adam Smith saw. The United States system is a **mixed economy**. In a mixed economy, the government has some control. Not all businesses are privately owned. Electric companies, for example, are sometimes owned by the public. Who owns the local school or the town library? Everyone does. Public ownership is sometimes mixed with private ownership.

mixed economy
a capitalist economy in which the government plays a limited role

The American economy is not always competitive. Some companies get so big that they choke off competition. At one time, Standard Oil controlled more than 90 percent of the oil business. The oil business was still capitalist. That is, Standard Oil was privately owned. However, there was no competition. In cases such as this, the government steps in to restore competition. Standard Oil was broken up into smaller companies. The same thing happened in the telephone business. Now we have many companies competing to provide our long-distance phone service.

In a mixed economy, the government sometimes steps in to break up monopolies or to give help to a company or an industry.

Does the government help private industry? In theory, a capitalist company should get no help from the state. In practice, however, the state often helps private industry. For one thing, the government is the nation's largest consumer. The state also passes tax laws that help business.

Sometimes the government gives help directly to businesses. The United States government promised more than $100 million in loans to Chrysler Corporation, the auto company. Without this help, Chrysler would have gone out of business. The government also helps farmers. The government promises farmers that they will get a certain price for their crops. This price is usually higher than the price set by the market.

Critical Thinking
What reasons might the government have to help a large corporation that is in financial trouble?

Understanding What You Read

1. What is capitalism?
2. What was Adam Smith's idea?
3. What is the invisible hand of the market? How does it work?
4. What is the difference between selling drugs in a drugstore and selling drugs on a street corner? Which of these actions is free enterprise? Explain.

Workbook Activities

Chapter Test, p. 12
Understanding the Free Enterprise System, p. 13

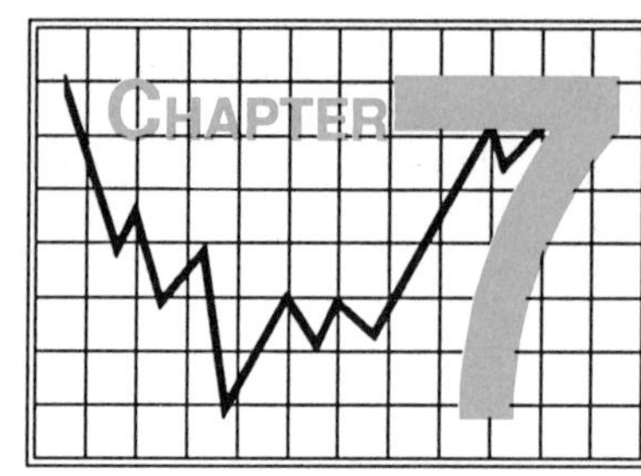

The Economy Flows in a Circle

Everyone in America is part of the American economic system. There is no escaping it. Everyone is a consumer. Everyone is also a seller. In the American economic system, people depend on each other.

division of labor
a method of production in which a task is divided into parts and different people do different parts of the task

What is the division of labor? Suppose that you are a shoemaker. How long would it take you to make a pair of shoes all by yourself? Surely it would take many hours. Working by yourself is usually not efficient. There is a faster way to get things done. When a job is divided into small tasks, a group of people can do different parts of the same job. This is called **division of labor** (duh-VIZH-un of LAY-bur).

With division of labor, several people make a pair of shoes. No one person makes a whole shoe. Each person has a separate task. One person cuts the leather. Another does the stitching. Each person does one task over and over.

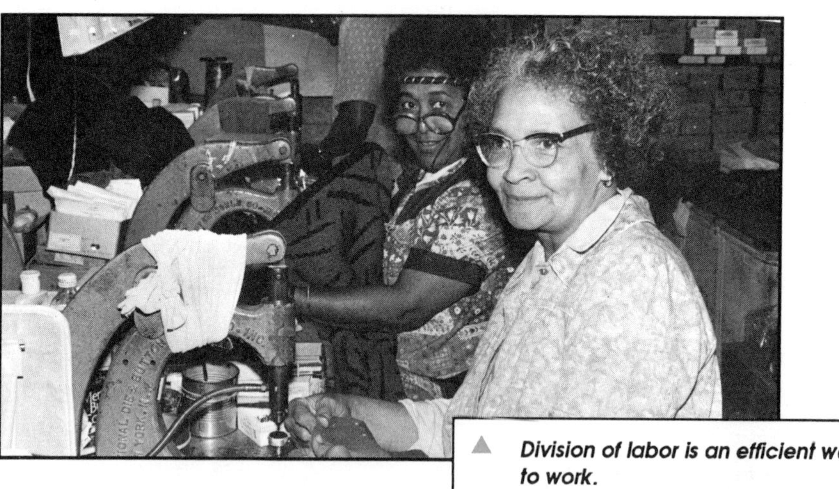

Division of labor is an efficient way to work.

Division of labor allows workers to produce more goods with less work.

One person working alone might take a day to make a pair of shoes. Three people working together might be able to make six pairs of shoes in one day. Because the work is divided, three people can make more shoes with less work.

How do workers benefit? All factories today use division of labor. No one person makes a whole car or toaster oven. Each person in an auto factory has special tasks. This system is good for two reasons. First, the workers can be trained more easily. They have to learn to do only a limited number of things. Second, the workers need fewer skills. For example, instead of learning how to make every part of a car, an auto worker learns how to make just one or two parts.

With division of labor, workers can be trained more easily because they need to learn fewer skills.

The division of labor makes modern life possible. Everyone does his or her small part. When all these small parts are added up, the economy produces the great wealth America has today.

People pay a price for all this efficiency, however. Division of labor means that people lose some of their independence. They need other people to make their shoes. They need other people to grow their food. Other people must pick up their garbage. Division of labor makes people more dependent on each other.

There is another problem with division of labor. It can be boring. Doing the same thing over and over can get pretty dull. Today smart managers understand this, and they look for ways to make the work more interesting.

What is the multiplier effect? People also depend on each other to spend money. Everyone has to spend a little in order to earn a little. Suppose that you spend three dollars for a half dozen bagels. The three dollars you spend becomes income for the owner of the bakery. Suppose that the bakery owner spends the three dollars to rent a movie. The same three dollars would then become income for the video store owner, who might spend it on a sandwich or a magazine. Your three dollars has been spent many times. Economists call this the **multiplier effect** (MUL-tih-ply-ur uh-FEKT).

multiplier effect
economic rule that one extra dollar in the economy will produce five dollars worth of spending

Suppose that someone decided to save your three dollars. This would end the multiplier effect. Saving can be good for individuals but bad for the economy as a whole. If too much money is being saved, the economy slows down.

Economists say that five dollars of additional spending is created by every dollar that is spent. That dollar's effect on the economy is multiplied by five because the dollar will change hands about five times before someone decides to save it. This is very important. If a company builds a $5 million plant in your town, it creates $25 million worth of spending.

The multiplier effect stops when someone saves the dollar.

What is the flow of resources? Figure 1 shows the flow of resources from individuals to businesses. Figure 1 also shows the flow of goods and

Money (resources) flows from individuals to businesses. Goods and services flow from businesses to individuals.

services from businesses to individuals. The American system is based largely on private ownership. The factors of production—land, labor, capital and management—are mostly in private hands.

real goods
goods produced by businesses using the factors of production

Businesses must buy the factors of production. They must pay a wage for your labor. They must pay for the land they put their buildings on. Businesses must also pay interest on the capital they borrow to start the company. The businesses then use these factors of production—the land, labor, capital and management—to produce goods and services. These goods produced by business are called **real goods** (REEL GOODZ).

The Flow of Real Goods

Figure 1

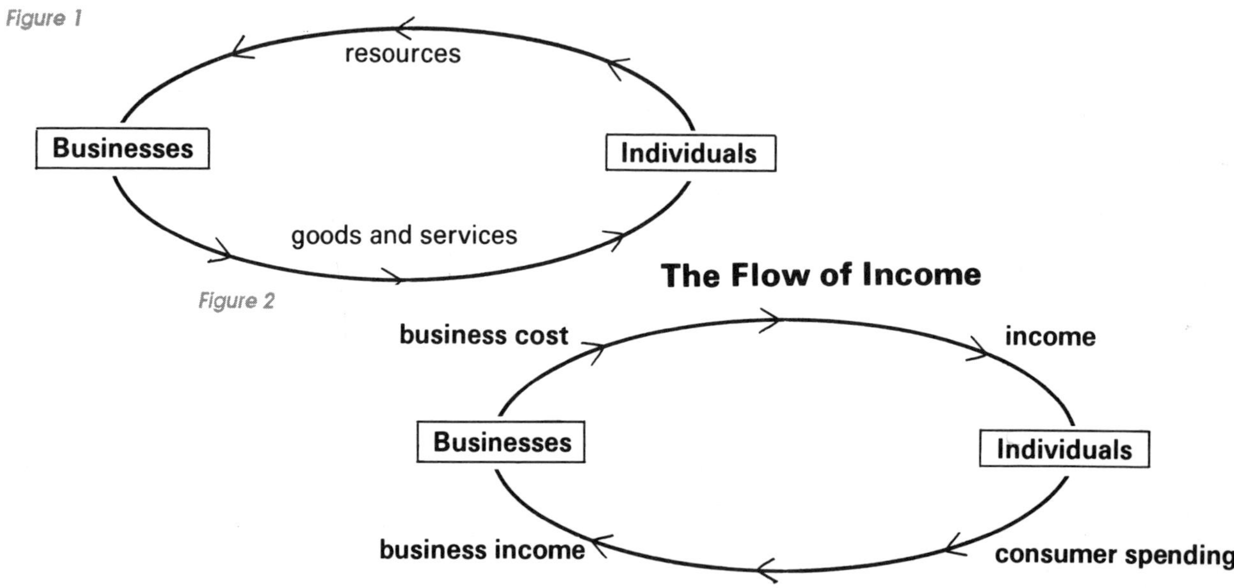

The Flow of Income

Figure 2

consumer spending
the flow of income in an economy that results when businesses pay workers and workers spend their income, creating profit for business and continuing the cycle

Figure 2 shows the flow of income, or money. Businesses pay for the factors of production. This is a cost to businesses. However, the money paid by businesses is income to the workers and the providers of capital and land. On the other hand, these same workers and providers must pay for the goods and services they consume. This is called **consumer spending** (kon-SOO-mur SPEND-ing). Consumer spending becomes income for the businesses selling these goods and services.

What is the flow of real goods and income? Figure 3 shows the flow of real goods and income. If the flow is in balance, there is no problem. If one part stops, they all stop.

The flow of real goods and income must be in balance for the economy to be healthy.

The flow of real goods and income is not always in balance. If consumer spending slows down, the flow of resources to business slows. A slower flow of resources to business means less income for individuals. Consumer spending drops, which means less income for business.

Figure 3

The Flow of Income and Real Goods

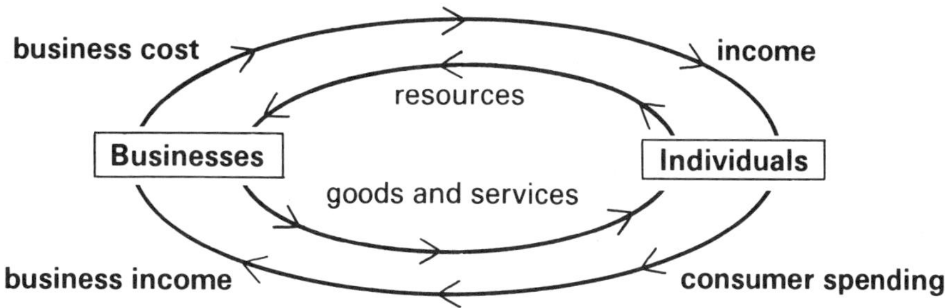

On Your Way Up
Review
After you finish reading this chapter, write a summary of the way in which real goods, income and savings and investments flow in the economy. Write the summary in your own words so you will remember it.

Figure 4

Savings and Investments

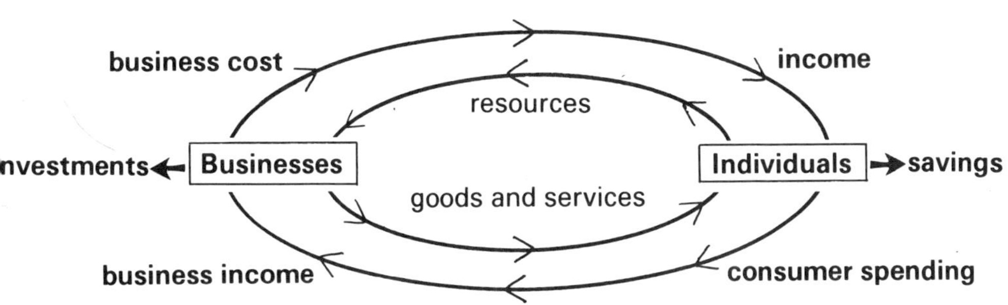

What about savings and investment? In Figure 4, not all the income is spent. Some of it has been drained off in savings. Savings can throw the economy off balance. However, businesses invest in new capital goods. If this investment equals the savings, the flow is again in balance.

Critical Thinking
Is it always a good idea for a person to save money?

What is the role of government? The role of government belongs on all of these charts. The government taxes and spends. If the taxing and spending are equal, the flow remains stable.

The government has an important role in the American economy.

Understanding What You Read

1. How does the division of labor affect the way goods are made?
2. Explain the multiplier effect.
3. What are real goods?
4. What happens if consumer spending slows down?

Workbook Activities

Chapter Test, p. 14
Reading a Bar Graph, p. 15

Empower Yourself - Cooperative Learning

Look at the chart that your group drew up for the Empower Yourself project. What item did you select as the best buy?

Write a brief explanation of why you all chose that item. Discuss the cost of the item. Was it the least expensive model? Mention any special features that you liked. Tell what features you would not need. Explain what you learned about being a smart shopper.

Review

Fill In On a separate sheet of paper, write the word or phrase that best completes each sentence.

1. The __________ is whatever a consumer cannot have because he or she has spent resources on something else.
2. The study of how and why goods are made and used is __________.
3. The exchange of one product for another product is called __________.
4. The effort of two or more sellers to attract the business of a buyer by offering the most favorable terms is called __________.
5. An extra benefit, such as a bonus, that encourages workers to work harder or more efficiently is called __________.
6. A money or goods from which income is earned is called __________.
7. People who combine land, labor and capital to produce goods and services are called__________.
8. The complete ownership of a market by one seller is called __________.
9. A refusal by consumers to buy a product or a service is a __________.
10. A __________ is a capitalist economy in which government plays a limited role.
11. An economic system based on private ownership of money is __________.
12. The economic rule that one dollar in the economy will produce five dollars worth of spending is known as the __________.
13. A measure of how efficiently workers are working is __________..
14. A good that may be used over and over time is a__________.
15. Land, labor, capital and management are the__________.
16. The use of__________allows a person to buy something with the promise to pay later.
17. The amount charged for a loan is called __________.
18. The __________means that different people do different parts of a job.
19. Adam Smith wrote__________.
20. People must have __________ in order to live.

How the United States Economy Works

Apartment owners compete in the marketplace for renters.

Empower Yourself - Cooperative Learning

Apartment owners compete for housing dollars. Form a group of five members. Find the listing of apartments in your local newspaper. Divide the listings into five categories by the cost of monthly rental: \$250-\$400, \$400-\$600, \$600-\$800, \$800-\$1,000 and more than \$1,000.

Each member of the group will choose a rent category and investigate two apartments that rent for amounts in that category. Look at the apartments in person or speak to the real estate agent who has the listing. Ask: How close is the nearest public transportation? Where are the nearest shopping areas? How many rooms does the apartment have? Does the building have a laundry room? If the apartment is above the second floor, is there an elevator? Is the apartment in good condition?

Get together with the other members of the group. Make a booklet with a separate information sheet for each apartment you researched. Discuss with the group the reasons why the monthly rental was higher for some apartments than for others.

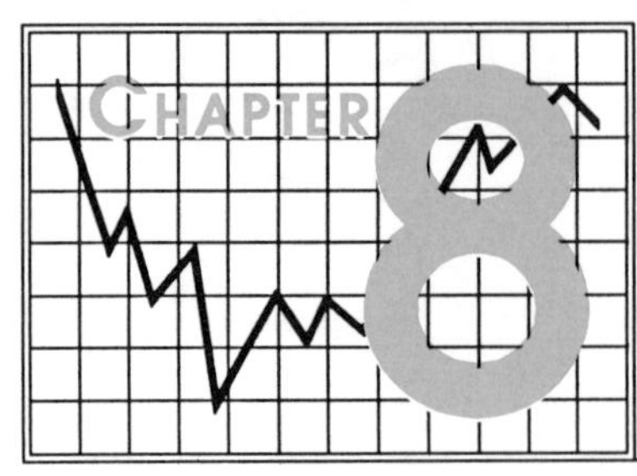

The Marketplace

demand
the amount of a good or service that consumers are willing to buy at all possible prices at a given time

supply
the amount of goods and services producers are willing to sell at all possible prices at a given time

Demand sets prices. When demand is low, prices drop. When demand is high, prices go up.

The marketplace is at the heart of the economy. The buyer meets the seller in the marketplace. The buyer tries to buy goods at the lowest possible price. The seller tries to sell goods at the highest possible price. The buyer represents **demand** (duh-MAND). The seller represents **supply** (suh-PLY). The buyer and the seller are not after the same thing. This difference in interests sets prices.

What does demand do? Demand helps to set prices. When demand is high, the price will probably be high. When demand is low, prices usually drop. People tend to buy more when prices fall because people are able to buy more at lower prices. On the other hand, people tend to buy less when prices rise. They might, for example, buy a lobster at $5 a pound. But how many lobsters would they buy at $15 a pound?

What changes demand? Demand changes with price. The result is a demand curve. Figure 1 shows the demand for lobsters at different prices. Notice the slope of the line. At $5 a pound, 400 lobsters are bought. When the price goes up to $10 a pound, only 200 lobsters are bought. When the price goes up to $15 a pound, sales drop off to only 100 lobsters.

> **How to Read a Line Graph**
> Line graphs, like bar graphs, are used to show information. First, look at the title. It will tell you what the graph measures. Then check the horizontal axis (the line at the bottom) and the vertical axis (the line at the left). Find out what each axis represents. The position of the line shows you whether the quantities on the chart are increasing or decreasing.

Figure 1

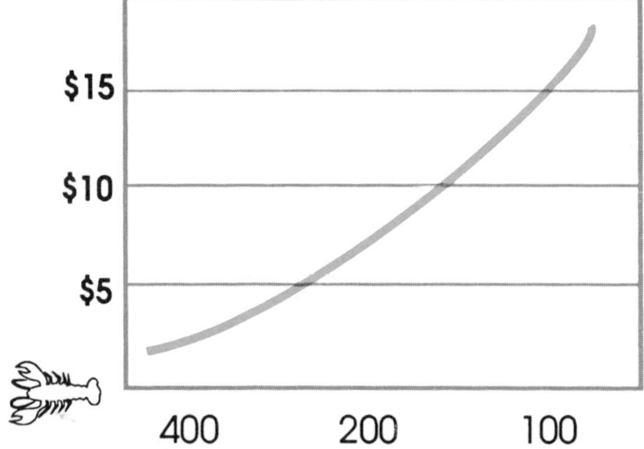

What affects demand? Demand can change for reasons other than price. Suppose the price of lobster drops to only $1 a pound. If you love lobster, the price is unbeatable. However, there is just so much lobster a person can eat. You can have too much lobster.

Does income affect demand? Demand also changes with income. If your income goes up, you have more money to spend. You can buy more products. Income can also go down. Many people lost their jobs in the early 1990s. For these people, demand changed because they could no longer afford to buy some things.

Can demand for one product affect another? Demand for one product can change demand for another product. If the price of gasoline suddenly doubles, what happens to the demand for large cars? The demand goes down. The demand for small cars goes up.

What is elastic demand? The demand for most products varies with price. When the price goes up, the demand goes down. This is called **elastic demand** (uh-LAS-tik duh-MAND). Figure 1 shows a demand curve that is elastic. When the price of lobster goes up, people buy less. When the price goes down, people will buy more.

What is inelastic demand? There are some products that people will buy at almost any price. This is called **inelastic demand** (IN-uh-las-tik duh-MAND). When the price goes up, the demand stays the same. Products with an inelastic demand have two main features. First, they have no close substitute. People cannot change to something that is almost the same. Second, people really need the product. Milk is a good example. Children need milk. There is no close substitute. If the price of milk doubles, most parents will still buy it for their children. Figure 2 shows a demand curve that is inelastic.

Figure 2

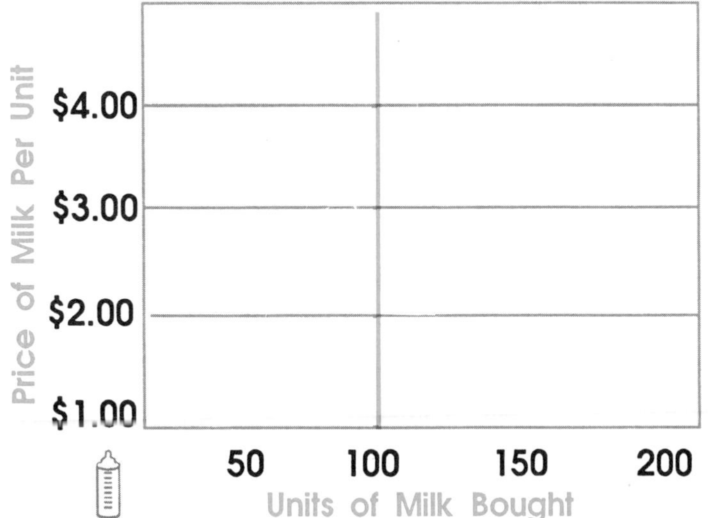

On Your Way Up
Fact and Opinion
A fact states something that can be proved. An opinion is a belief that someone feels. "Demand can change" is a fact. What is an opinion? Is the last sentence in the first paragraph on this page a fact?

Critical Thinking
If the price of butter doubled, how would the demand for margarine be affected?

elastic demand
a demand that varies with price

inelastic demand
demand that does not change with price

What affects supply? Sellers also react to price changes. But their reaction is opposite the reaction of buyers. The higher the price, the more sellers are willing and able to sell. The lower the price, the less they are willing and able to sell. Supply is not fixed. It equals the amount of goods and services offered for sale at all possible prices. Suppose the price of oil is $15 a barrel. Most sellers say that price is too low. Few wells stay in use. The supply of oil will drop. Suppose the price goes up to $25 a barrel. Some wells will go back into production at this higher price. If the price of oil goes up to $35 a barrel, the wells will be worth running.

When prices are high, sellers are willing to increase supply. When prices are low, supply decreases.

What is a supply curve? Figure 3 shows a normal supply curve. Notice that it is the opposite of the demand curve. When oil is only $15 a barrel, most sellers just let the oil stay in the ground. When higher prices come along, they will pump the oil out of the ground.

Figure 3

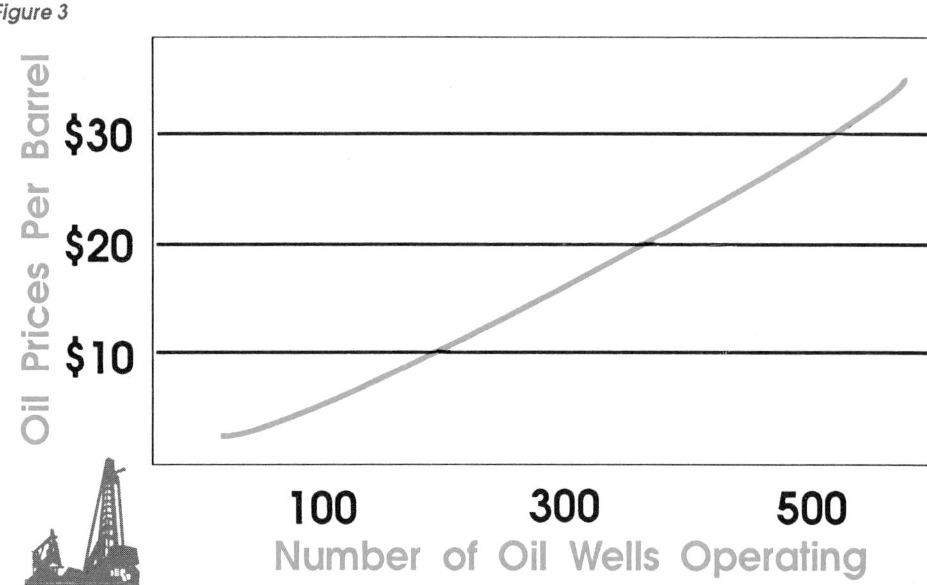

The supply of something, such as land or gold, is fixed.

The same supply curve applies to human labor. How many people will mow grass for $2 an hour? For $10 an hour? For $50 an hour? The law of supply is direct. As the price goes up, the supply goes up.

A few things do not fit this law of supply. The supply of some things is fixed. The supply of land is fixed. So is the world's supply of gold. These items have a supply that is inelastic.

Critical Thinking

How did the assembly line affect the supply of cars?

What other factors affect supply? Factors other than price may affect supply. Supply may also be affected by finding better ways to do things. Look at Figure 4. The old supply curve (S) shows 200 units offered at $20. Then a new and better way of making the product is found. Now there is a new supply curve (S1). Here sellers are willing and able to offer $400 units at $15.

Figure 4

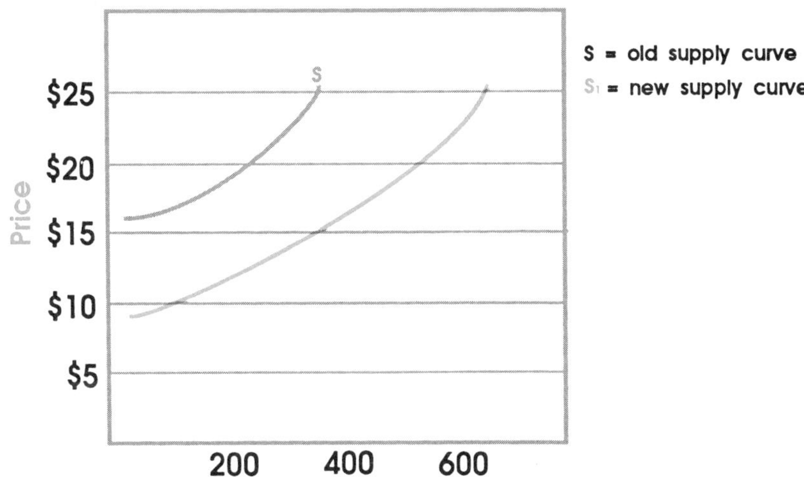

Does supply ever meet demand? How do the demand curve and the supply curve fit together? Figure 5 shows where supply meets demand. In Figure 5, the demand curve (D) meets the supply curve (S) at point 1. Point 1 makes both the buyers and the sellers happy. Their desires are in balance. The sellers will produce 300 units at $15 each. At point 2, however, there is not enough demand. The price of $25 is too high for most buyers. At point 3, there is not enough supply. The price of $10 is too low for most sellers. The prices are set by the forces of supply and demand.

Figure 5

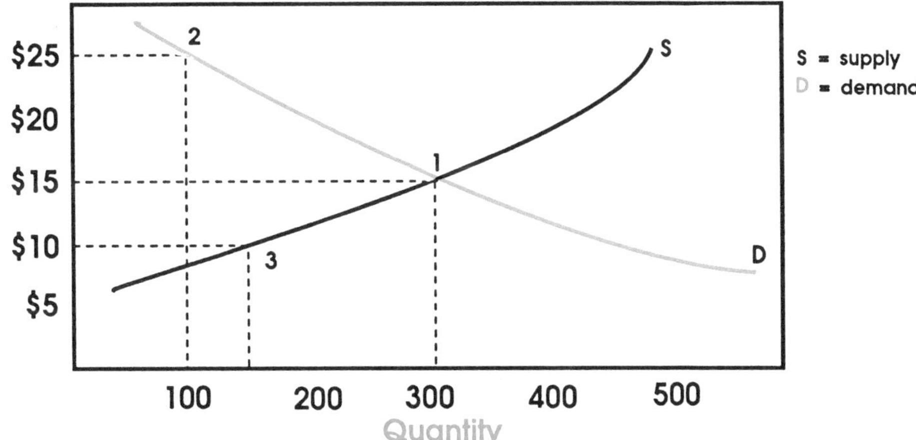

When supply meets demand, the desires of buyers and sellers are in balance.

Understanding What You Read

1. What is demand?
2. What is supply?
3. Explain the difference between elastic and inelastic demand.
4. What is a supply curve?
5. What happens when supply meets demand?

Workbook Activities

Chapter Test, p. 16
Critical Thinking, p. 17

Profits

The marketplace runs on profits. Sellers enter the marketplace because they want to make money. This desire to make money is called the profit motive (PRAHF-it MOH-tiv). The profit motive is a very important part of the economy.

On Your Way Up
Main Idea
The main idea of a paragraph is the sentence that tells you what the paragraph is about. The main idea is usually stated in the first or last sentence of a paragraph. Look for the main idea sentence in each paragraph in this chapter. Write each main idea sentence in your notes for use as a study guide.

What is the role of profits? Profit is what is left over after all the expenses have been paid. The owner pays for the land, the labor and the capital—the factors of production. The rest is profit. However, something is missing in this definition. What about management? Management is also a factor of production. Management, therefore, is a cost, just like land, labor and capital. The money an owner pays himself or herself is part of the cost of doing business. Profit is the difference between total income and total costs.

Profits are earned, just as wages are earned. Profits are the reward for taking risks. No one who starts a new business can be sure of making a profit. Too many things can go wrong. An owner can lose money. Even huge companies like Chrysler, U.S. Steel and Pan American have lost money. Companies can lose money for many different reasons. One reason is the consumer's decision to buy from someone else who offers a better product or lower prices.

Critical Thinking
What will happen to a business if the owner pays himself or herself too much money?

Management, labor, land and capital are all costs. Profit is the difference between total income and total costs.

Pan American went out of business in 1992 because it lost too much money.

What risks do owners take? The marketplace is always changing. No owner of a business can control a free marketplace. An owner cannot tell people what or when to buy. People's tastes change all the time. What they bought last year, they may not buy this year.

Owners must take risks. Bad economic conditions and wrong guesses about the consumer can cause a business to fail.

Owners face the risk of hard times. People may want to buy a product but not be able to afford it. Suppose that you own a bicycle shop in a factory town. If the factory closes down, most of the people in town will be out of work. How many bicycles will you be able to sell? This is just one example of how times can change. Hard times are a risk every owner must take.

What kinds of profits are there? There are two basic kinds of profits. They are called **normal profits** (NOR-mul PRAHF-its) and **excess profits** (EK-ses PRAHF-its). Normal profits must cover all costs plus a profit for the owner. If a normal profit is not earned, the business cannot continue.

normal profits
the lowest profits that will keep a business going

excess profits
money earned over and above normal profits

There is no exact dollar amount that equals normal profit. Normal profit varies from business to business and from owner to owner. If the owner does not make normal profits, he or she will find something else to do. The owner will find work that either pays more or has fewer risks.

Excess profit is the money earned over and above normal profits. Excess profits are not needed to keep a business going. In a free market, excess profits usually do not last very long. When people will see how much money there is to be made, they will enter the market. Suppose a taco stand is making excess profits because it is the only taco stand in town. Sooner or later, someone else will open a competing taco stand. There go the excess profits! That is the way the market system works.

Excess profits do not last long because they invite competition.

Look at Figure 1. Line A is the normal profit line. It was made thick to remind you that there is no exact dollar amount. A company at line A will stay in business. Anything above line A represents excess profits. Profits in that area will make others want to enter the field. On the other hand, a company below line A makes no profit. It will soon go out of business.

Figure 1

What does the profit motive do? The profit motive plays a large role in the economy. The need for profits forces managers to think ahead. They cannot rest on what they did yesterday. Managers must always come up with new ideas to increase profits. If they do not, others will grab the profits tomorrow.

The profit motive makes owners use their resources in the way that makes the most money.

Suppose that Company A and Company B make skateboards. Company A is making profits now, but it has no future plans. Management is not putting profits back into the company to make it grow. There are no plans for new products or no new investments. Company B, on the other hand, is losing money for the moment. But it has big plans. Management plans to invest in a new style skateboard. The company hopes that consumers will like the new style, which will earn future profits.

Which company is taking a risk? Both companies are taking a risk. Company A is taking the risk of doing nothing. It could lose its customers who want something new. Company B is taking the risk that its new skateboard might fail. But Company B's new skateboard might be a smash hit. In that case, its future profits could be great as it wins customers away from Company A. On the other hand, Company A's decision to do nothing might force it out of the skateboard business.

Critical Thinking
What might make a business put the needs of the environment above the desire to make money?

Does profit affect the use of resources? Resources are scarce. People must make choices. Will a piece of land be used for farming or will it be used to build a shopping mall? Often the decision depends on which would make the most money. People often place the desire to make money above the need to protect the land, air and water.

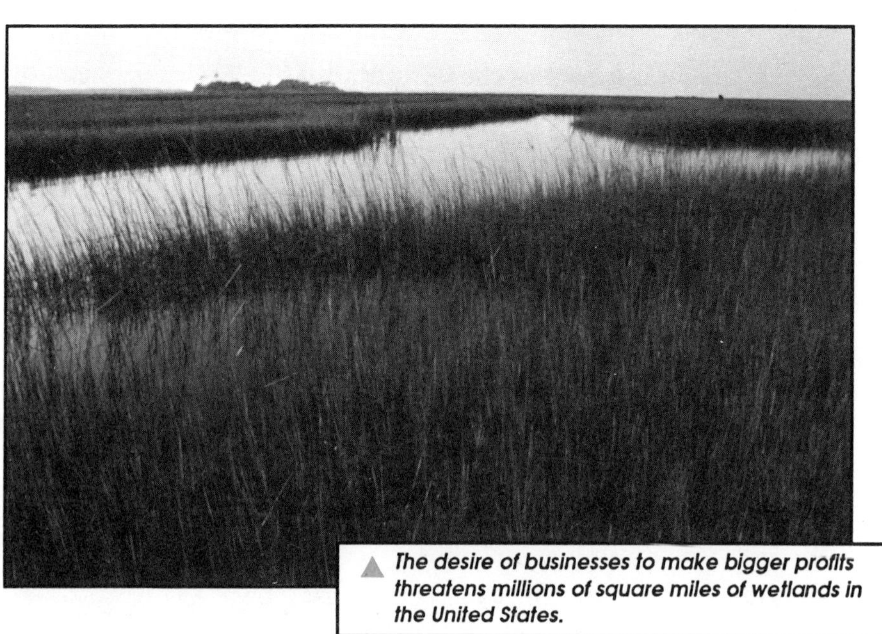

The desire of businesses to make bigger profits threatens millions of square miles of wetlands in the United States.

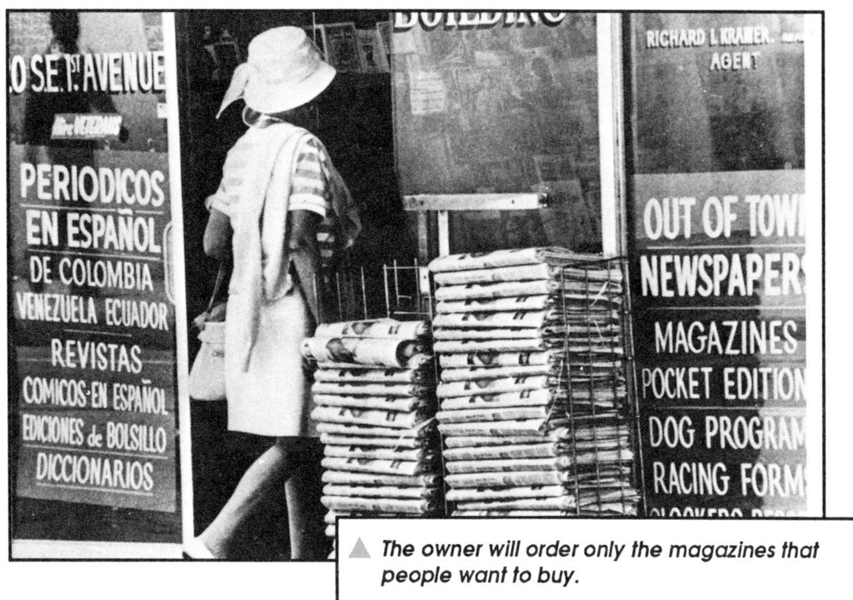

The owner will order only the magazines that people want to buy.

How does profit affect sellers? The profit motive forces an owner to give you—the buyer—what you want. The owner of a magazine stand orders many magazines. If some of them do not sell, the owner stops ordering them. The owner can make profits only from the magazines that are sold.

The profit motive forces owners to give consumers what they want.

Profits make the marketplace work. Profits force people to plan ahead and to invest more in their businesses. Profits encourage people to develop new ideas and better ways of doing things. Profits affect the ways that people use—and misuse—resources. Profits tell the seller what the buyer wants.

Understanding What You Read

1. What is profit?
2. What is the difference between normal profits and excess profits?
3. Why do excess profits not last long?
4. What risks do owners take?
5. How does profit affect the use of resources?

Workbook Activities

Chapter Test, p. 18
Interpreting a Line Graph, p. 19

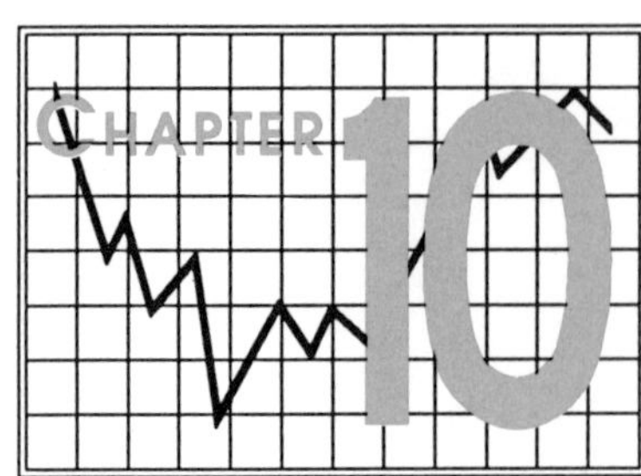

Chapter 10 Competition

On Your Way Up
Review
Review Chapters 3 and 4. Then write a paragraph about the ways in which competition affects consumers and producers.

Free enterprise is the right to enter a market freely. When many people enter a market, several things happen as a result of competition. In a competitive market, prices are low and quality is high. The buyer has a wide range of choices. Buyers who do not like the crust at one pizza stand will go elsewhere. People who make the best pizza for the lowest price stay in business. Businesses that fall short in either quality or price will fail.

With pure competition, there are many sellers and many buyers.

What is the nature of competition? Competition is a contest. There are winners and losers. Each seller is out to make money. The tasks are to produce and to sell. Human values, such as love or friendship, are not part of the game. No one really cares how nice a person is or how many children he or she has to support. The rules of competition are simple. Success is rewarded, and failure is punished.

pure competition
a market in which no one can control the supply or the demand

What is pure competition? A large number of buyers and a large number of sellers create **pure competition** (PYOOR kom-puh-TIH-shun). In such a market, no one can control the supply or the demand. No one can control the price. The choice made by a few buyers does not change the market. Neither does the choice made by a few sellers.

The pizza business is an example of pure competition. Starting a pizza stand takes money, but it does not take huge amounts. Many people can go into this business. It seems as if every street corner in America has a pizza stand. Most people like pizza. There are many buyers and many sellers. That is why there is so much competition in the pizza business. The same is true of most small businesses.

When there is pure competition, no one can control supply or demand.

Are some industries less competitive than others? Many industries are not like the pizza business. In some cases, a few companies control the whole industry. Auto makers are a good example. There are only a few auto makers in the United States. Steel makers are another example. U.S. Steel and Bethlehem Steel, the two huge American steel makers, compete against each other. Even so, they still dominate the market. Their real competition comes from nations such as Japan and Germany.

In industries where there is little competition, companies can more easily control supply.

There is not much competition in the steel industry.

What makes the car or steel business different from most small businesses? The answer is cost. Making cars or steel costs great sums of money—billions of dollars. Such companies are not begun by individual business people.

What is the role of advertising? Another difference between small and large businesses is the amount they spend on advertising. Most pizza stands spend very little money on advertising. The owners might run a newspaper ad or they might buy some radio time. But for the most part, small companies have small ads.

Critical Thinking
How do advertisers create needs?

Big companies are different. They can create demand by telling the buyer what he or she wants. This is the heart of advertising. Big companies spend huge sums on advertising in order to create demand. Some companies are willing to spend hundreds of thousands of dollars just for a 30-second ad during the Super Bowl or the World Series. Many billions of dollars are spent every year by American companies on advertisements. Big companies know that to compete, they must advertise. They must not only sell the buyer what the buyer needs, but they must create new needs.

Big companies use advertising to create demand.

Companies must also respond to needs consumers develop on their own. For example, many consumers now want less fat in their food. Fast-food restaurants have gotten the message. They now offer consumers lean hamburgers, "lite" chicken and green salads.

Critical Thinking
What would the government do if an auto maker tried to buy up all the other auto companies?

What is the role of government? At one time, Standard Oil of Ohio controlled more than 90 percent of the oil business. Standard Oil controlled the supply of oil, and Standard Oil controlled the price of oil. Finally, the government stepped in and broke up Standard Oil into several smaller companies. Why was this done? The government wanted to restore competition.

The government breaks up large companies when they try to become so powerful that no one can compete with them.

Under the law, the government can prevent companies from trying to become so powerful that no other company can compete with them. Alcoa—the aluminum giant—was divided into four companies. Recently, AT&T, the telephone company, was forced to break up. Some people question whether such break-ups are in the consumer's best interest. A court case involved in breaking up a giant company often takes years. Is it worth the cost? Do break-ups help or hurt the public in the long run? Will they lead to better goods and services? There are no clear answers to these questions.

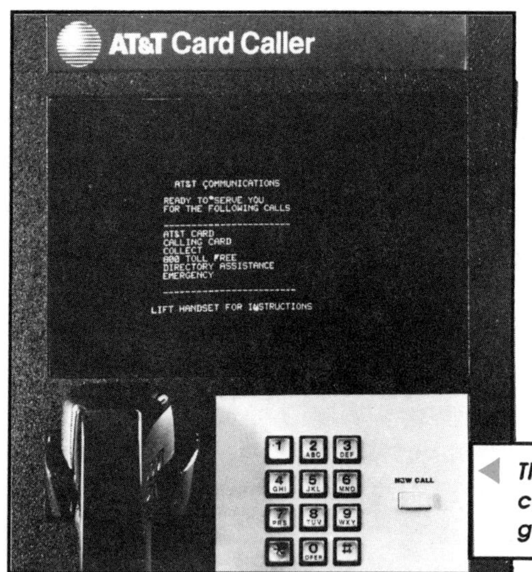

The government breaks up companies when they try to get too powerful.

The government allows monopolies when they are in the public interest. Public utilities are among the monopolies that are allowed by law.

Does the government ever allow monopolies? In a few cases, the government allows monopolies. A monopoly is the control of a market by one company. One case of monopoly is a public utility. Public utilities provide such services as gas and electricity, transportation and water to cities. Having competition for these services does not make sense. What city needs five power companies? State governments set up one legal monopoly for each such service. This monopoly is outside the marketplace. Competition does not set the price. The government does. The prices charged by all public utilities must be approved by the state government.

Sometimes a monopoly can be in the best interest of the people.

What are the levels of competition? The chart below shows the levels of competition in the American economy. In some fields, the competition is pure. There are many buyers and many sellers. No one pizza maker or auto mechanic can control the industry. In big industries, such as auto making and steel, there are far fewer sellers. There is less free enterprise because it is so hard for new sellers to enter the market. Companies at this level have the power to create demand by developing and promoting a new product. On the third level, there is no competition. Here the government allows monopolies. However, these monopolies are closely watched by the government.

Free enterprise increases as competition increases.

Levels of Competition

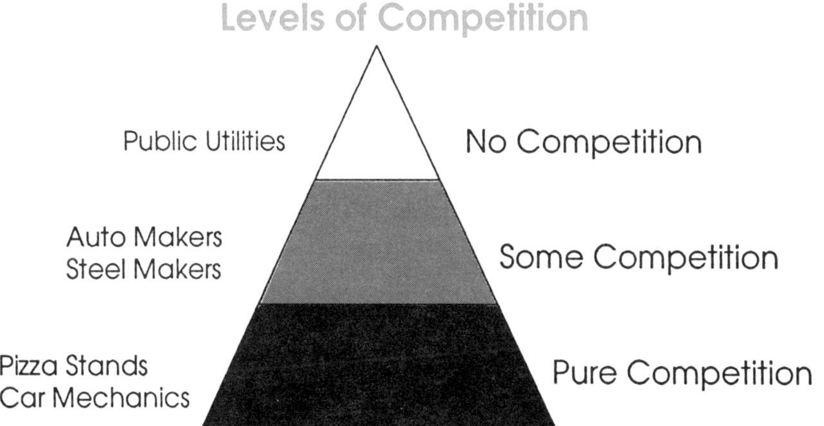

Understanding What You Read

1. What happens to prices and quality when a market is competitive?
2. What is pure competition?
3. How does advertising affect competition?
4. Why did the government break up Standard Oil?
5. Why does the government allow some monopolies?

Workbook Activities

Chapter Test, p. 20
Comparing Circle Graphs, p. 21

Inflation

When the cost of a favorite product goes up, people often blame inflation. But, is it inflation when the Boston Red Sox increase ticket prices by a dollar? Is it inflation if the electric bill jumps by 15 percent? In each case, the answer is no.

Not all price increases are the result of inflation. Some increases are caused by changes in supply or demand.

What is inflation? A rise in cost of one or two or even three items is not inflation (in-FLAY-shun). Inflation is a rise in the overall level of prices. The cost of living (kost of LIV-ing), which is the price of most goods and services, has to be going up, not just the cost of one thing. Likewise, deflation (dee-FLAY-shun) is not just a drop in gas prices. It is a drop in the overall cost of goods and services.

What affects prices? Seasonal supply can affect prices. Lettuce is in greater supply in June than in December. For this reason, the price is lower in June and higher in December. Demand can also affect prices. A successful ball team can charge more for tickets than a losing team.

With inflation, the prices of almost all goods and services go up.

Which prices rise with inflation? To have inflation, almost all the prices have to go up. There is no inflation if half the prices go up and half the prices go down by the same amount. You have inflation if the cost of food is going up *and* the cost of entertainment is going up *and* the cost of heating your home is going up.

With inflation, the dollar does not buy what it once did. Figure 1 shows how fast a 15 percent **rate of inflation** (RAYT of in-FLAY-shun) destroys the buying power of a dollar.

rate of inflation
a percentage that shows how fast the dollar is losing its value

Figure 1

The Shrinking Dollar
(at 15% annual inflation)

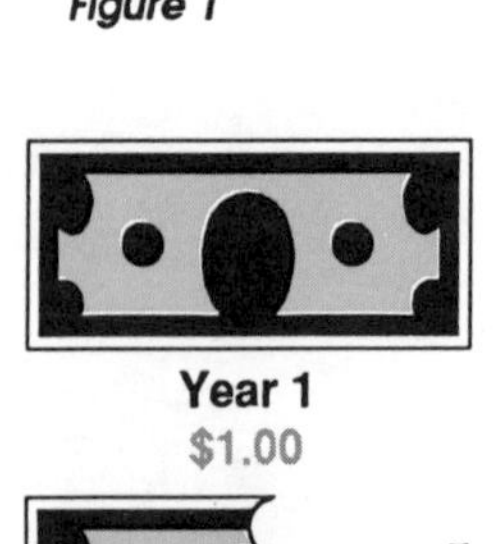

Year 1
$1.00

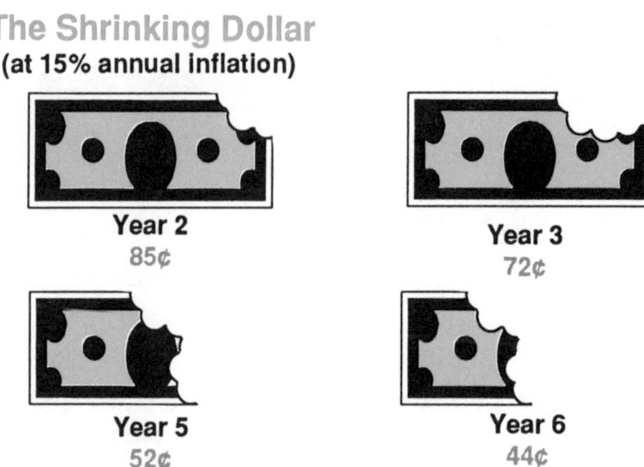

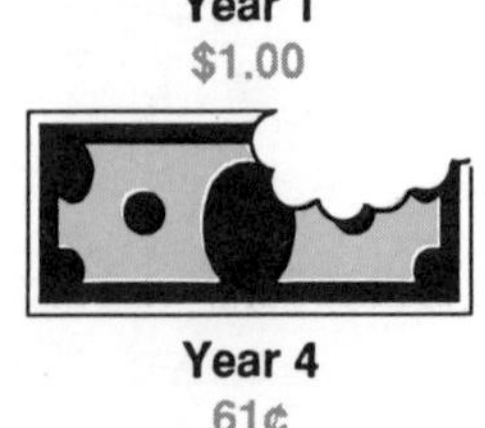

Year 4
61¢

Naturally, most people do not like inflation. However, small increases in inflation of about 3 percent or 4 percent a year do not hurt too much. A little inflation is often a sign of a healthy, growing economy. Deflation, on the other hand, seems good. But in almost every case, deflation comes only where there is no growth and unemployment is high.

While a little inflation may be all right, too much inflation clearly is not. High inflation can destroy the value of your earnings. Runaway, or very high, inflation can destroy the economy of a nation.

What is the Consumer Price Index? The most popular measure of inflation is the Consumer Price Index (kon-SOO-mur PRYS IN-deks). The Consumer Price Index (CPI) measures how the cost of goods and services changes. The CPI measures changes in the cost of such things as food, clothing, housing, medicine and transportation. The change is stated as a percent. If the CPI shows 10 percent yearly increase, you will need $1.10 to buy what $1.00 bought a year before. Look at the CPI table below. Notice which prices have risen the most in the past few years.

How to Read the Consumer Price Index

The Consumer Price Index measures inflation. A CPI table shows how the prices of different items have increased or decreased. Look at the CPI table below. The base year is 1983. All the prices for that year equal 100. Fuel prices, for example, are listed at 100 for 1983. Prices before 1983 are almost always lower, so they are under 100. Prices after 1983 are higher, so they are over 100. If the CPI for a certain item is 200 in 1990, that means it cost twice as much in 1990 as it did in 1983.

Consumer Price Index

YEAR	ALL ITEMS	FOOD	TRANSPORTATION	HOUSING	FUEL	CLOTHING	MEDICAL CARE
1970	38.8	40.1	37.5	36.4	29.0	59.2	34.0
1975	53.5	60.2	50.1	50.7	45.0	72.5	47.5
1980	82.4	86.7	83.1	81.1	75.0	90.9	74.9
1983	100.0	100.0	100.0	100.0	100.0	100.0	100.0
1985	107.3	105.6	106.4	107.7	106.0	105.0	113.1
1987	113.6	113.5	105.4	114.2	103.0	110.6	130.1
1988	118.3	118.2	108.7	118.5	104.0	115.4	138.6
1989	124.0	124.9	114.1	123.0	107.0	118.6	149.3
1990	130.7	132.1	120.5	128.5	111.0	124.1	162.8

What are the two kinds of inflation? There are two basic kinds of inflation. One is called demand-pull (duh-MAND-PUL), or buyer's inflation. The other is called cost-push (KOST-PUSH), or seller's inflation.

Critical Thinking

Why is the cost of medical care rising?

Demand-pull inflation occurs when there is not enough supply to meet a rising demand.

What is demand-pull inflation? Demand-pull inflation occurs when demand goes up faster than supply. This causes an inflationary gap. The only way to fill the gap is to raise prices. People who scalp, or sell illegally, tickets at sporting events know this very well. Millions of people would like to see the Super Bowl in person. But no stadium has that much seating. There is a huge demand with a limited supply of tickets. That is why $60 tickets are scalped for $500 or more. This is the way demand-pull works.

Cost-push inflation occurs when the cost of making a product rises.

What is cost-push inflation? Cost-push inflation is a different story. In this case, inflation comes from supply. The cost of making a product or providing a service goes up. If auto workers get a raise, the price of cars goes up. The demand for cars does not cause the price increase. The demand stays more or less the same. However, the labor cost of making cars has gone up, so the price of cars has to go up. This is the way cost-push inflation works.

Every wage increase does not cause cost-push inflation. If a worker gets a 10 percent raise for being 10 percent more productive, there is no inflation. But if the worker gets a 10 percent raise for doing the same thing, there is inflation. Assume that a worker who produces 100 units an hour gets a 10% raise. If the worker now produces 110 units an hour, there is no inflation. The raise is balanced by increased production. If production stays at 100 units an hour, there is cost-push inflation.

price-wage spiral
a cycle in which increased wages result in increased prices, which result in a demand for increased wages, and so forth

Labor leaders often argue that workers need more pay to keep up with the cost of living. However, each round of increased wages means another round of increased prices. This is called a **price-wage spiral** (PRYS-WAYJ SPY-rul). Prices go up. Then wages go up. So prices go up again, and so forth. That is one reason why inflation occurs almost every year.

Who is hurt by inflation? Retired people living on pensions are hurt by inflation because they have fixed incomes (FIKST IN-kumz). Their income does not rise with inflation. Government workers are hurt because their salaries do not keep up with inflation. People who keep their money in savings accounts at a bank are hurt. Their balances increase, but the buying power of the money decreases. What good is it to earn 5 1/2 percent interest from a bank if the inflation rate is 15 percent? The only thing to do is to put your money where it will earn interest at least equal to the rate of inflation.

Savings accounts are not always the best place for a consumer's money. Smart savers watch interest rates.

Are banks hurt by inflation? The high inflation of the late 1970s and early 1980s nearly killed many banks. Banks are in the business of lending money. Banks charge interest for this service. The rate of this interest must be higher than the rate of inflation. Otherwise, the bank will lose money. Suppose the inflation rate is 2 1/2 percent and the bank charges 7 1/2 percent interest. In this case, the bank makes a 5 percent profit on loans.

In the 1970s, the banks lent money at 7 1/2 percent interest. Suddenly, inflation shot up to 12 1/2 percent. The banks lost 5 percent on their loans. That is not the way to stay in business. Today, banks often use adjustable interest rates. When inflation goes up, the banks' interest rate also goes up. This protects the banks against inflation.

A sudden increase in inflation can cause banks to pay out more money in interest than they collect from existing loans.

Who is helped by inflation? Inflation does not hurt everyone equally. Inflation raises the value of land and homes. Owners benefit when their property values increase faster than the overall rate of inflation. Renters are not so lucky. They do not own a home that is increasing in value. In general, low-income people, who often rent, are hurt more by inflation than high-income people, who often own property.

Critical Thinking

How does inflation affect the cost of renting an apartment? Explain.

People who owe money are sometimes helped by inflation. Suppose you borrow $1,000 at 7 1/2 percent interest, and inflation shoots up to 12 1/2 percent. Inflation makes the dollar you are paying back worth less than the dollar you borrowed. In this case, the 5 percent loss for the bank is your 5 percent gain.

Some young workers can also benefit from inflation. They are just beginning to climb up the salary or wage scale. They are more likely to get promotions or change jobs than older, more settled workers. As a result, their salaries or wages are more likely to keep pace with rising inflation. Compared to some older workers, young workers are getting richer. They are moving up while others are standing still. Inflation is not always bad for everyone. It hurts everyone in some way, but it can help certain people.

On Your Way Up

Organizing in a Chart

Make a chart with two columns. In the first column, list the kinds of people and businesses who are hurt by inflation. In the second column, list the kinds of people and businesses who are helped by inflation. Write a heading for each column in your chart.

Understanding What You Read

1. What is inflation?
2. What is deflation?
3. What does the rate of inflation show?
4. How does the wage-price spiral work?
5. How can inflation hurt banks?

Workbook Activities

Chapter Test, p. 22
Reading a Consumer Price Index, p. 23

Most people try to spend about one quarter of their yearly income on housing. Write down the monthly rent for each of the apartments you researched. Multiply that amount by 12—the number of months in a year. The answer will be the yearly cost of renting the apartments.

Multiply the yearly rentals by four. The answer will be the amount of income you would need to pay your rent on those apartments, as well as your food, clothing and other expenses.

A. On a separate sheet of paper, write the numbers from 1 to 10. Next to each number, write whether the statement below is True or False.

1. In the marketplace, the buyer represents demand.
2. Supply is the amount of a good or a service that consumers are willing to buy.
3. In the marketplace, the seller represents demand.
4. Demand helps to set price.
5. Supply is the amount of a good that producers are willing to sell.
6. Demand changes with price.
7. Demand cannot change with income.
8. Fashion can affect demand.
9. The demand for most products is inelastic.
10. The demand for products that people will buy at almost any price is called elastic demand.

B. On a separate sheet of paper, write the numbers from 1 to 6. Match each term in Column B with its description in Column A. Write the letter of the correct term next to the number on your paper.

Column A	Column B
1. the desire to make money	**a.** inelastic demand
2. the lowest profits that will keep a business going	**b.** normal profits
3. demand that does not change with price	**c.** inflation
4. demand that varies with price	**d.** profit motive
5. money earned over and above normal profits	**e.** supply
6. a rise in the overall level of prices	**g.** elastic demand
	h. excess profits

Wages, Labor and Taxes

Choosing a career, such as car sales, requires careful research.

Empower Yourself - Cooperative Learning

Choosing a career is one of the most important things you will ever do. Form a group of five members. Each member will choose a different occupation to research. Look for information about the job. Call employment agencies, labor unions or local job-training centers. Contact the career-planning centers in local colleges and universities.

Find out what training or education is needed to find a job in your chosen field. Ask how much time you would spend in training for the job. Discover what the entry-level salary is, and ask what the average person makes who holds that job. Find out if any special talents are needed to do the job.

With the members of the group, make a chart of the different occupations. Across the top of the chart, write the headings TRAINING/EDUCATION, TRAINING TIME, ENTRY-LEVEL SALARY, AVERAGE SALARY and SPECIAL TALENTS. Fill in the information for each occupation the group researched.

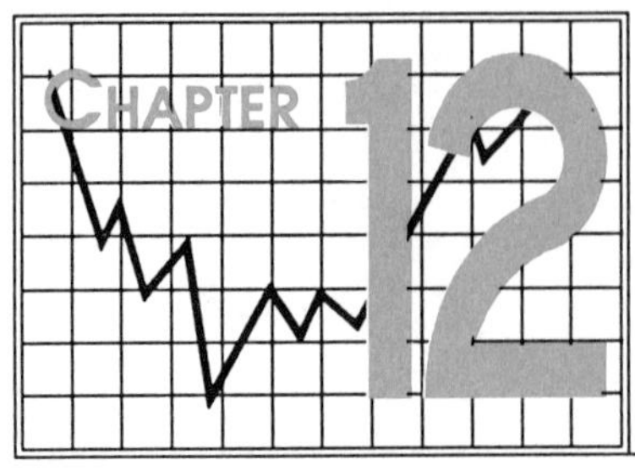

Wages

On Your Way Up
Preview
Before you read this unit, preview each chapter to find out what it will be about. Look for words in **bold** print in the paragraphs and in the margins. Read the questions that begin paragraphs and end each chapter. Look at the photos and illustrations. Read the captions. Predict what you will learn about in each chapter.

The price paid for any form of labor is called a wage (WAYJ). To the worker, this wage is income (IN-kum), or money received. To the employer, this wage is an expense (ek-SPENS), or money paid out for work. Of course, wages are not the same for all jobs. Some jobs pay much more than others. The reason for the difference in wages is supply and demand. For the most part, the marketplace sets wage rates in the United States. The employer "buys" the service of the worker. If many workers can supply the service, the wages will tend to be low. If only a few workers can supply the service, the wages will tend to be high.

wages in kind
noncash payments, such as room and board or meals

What kinds of wages are there? There are all kinds of wages. First, there is the wage a worker receives in his or her paycheck. That is one form of wage. Another form is **wages-in-kind**, or noncash payments. Wages-in-kind can be "free" room and board. People who work in resort hotels are often paid in this way. The room and board are not really free. They are part of the wage, and they have real value. You should think of them as income; your employer will certainly think of them as an expense. Your wages-in-kind plus your paycheck wages are called money wages.

regular wages
pay for a week's work of 35-40 hours

overtime pay
pay for work done above 40 hours

What are regular and overtime wages? Most workers are paid an hourly rate. If you work a part-time job at a fast-foods restaurant, you may earn $5 an hour. For a 20-hour week, your weekly wage will be $100. A full-time worker usually works an average of 40 hours a week. His or her **regular** weekly wage would be $200. Sometimes a worker will be asked to work more than 40 hours a week. When this happens, they earn **overtime** pay. Most often this is one and one half times their regular pay. At this rate, a person earning $5 an hour would earn $7.50 an hour in overtime pay.

Instead of earning regular wages, some people make a living on piecework wages or commissions.

What are piecework wages? Some workers are paid by the piece. Apple pickers are paid for each bushel they pick. Freelance writers are paid a certain amount for each article. Some factory workers are paid for each sneaker stitched. A wage based on the number of pieces produced is called **piecework**. The worker is paid a certain amount of money for each piece made. Sales workers are often paid a commission (kuh-MISH-un), or fee, based on the selling price of each item.

Some workers receive a **bonus** (BOH-nus). A bonus is paid when a certain worker does something special. Bonuses are most often given to managers who do their jobs very well. Some companies provide **profit sharing** (PRAHF-it SHAIR-ing). Profit-sharing companies give workers part of the profits the company makes. Some workers, such as teachers and army officers, are paid a **salary** (SAL-uh-ree). A salary is a wage paid over the course of the year. A salary is not affected by the number of hours a person works.

bonus
a special payment based on performance

profit sharing
a plan in which an employer gives the workers a part of the company's profits

salary
fixed pay for regular work

What are real wages? Money wages are different from real wages. What you make in money wages is not as important as what you can buy with those wages. Real wages are what your money will buy. Money wages always seem to be going up. Figure 1 shows the climb in yearly wages for people who work in mining, manufacturing and retail trade from 1980 to 1988. Miners, for example, went from about $23,500 in 1980 to about $35,000 in 1988. Retail workers are paid less than miners. The average yearly wage of retail workers rose from about $11,000 to about $15,000 from 1980 to 1988. Workers in manufacturing, as well as just about everyone else, saw their money wages go up during the 1980s. However, that does not mean that real wages were going up. In fact, for most people, real wages were going down!

Critical Thinking Suppose that your salary in 1985 was $10,000 and it is now $15,000. If inflation has gone up by 57 percent since 1985, have you gained or lost real wages? Explain.

Figure 1

YEARLY GROSS WAGES for Certain Occupations 1980 - 1989

(in thousands of dollars)

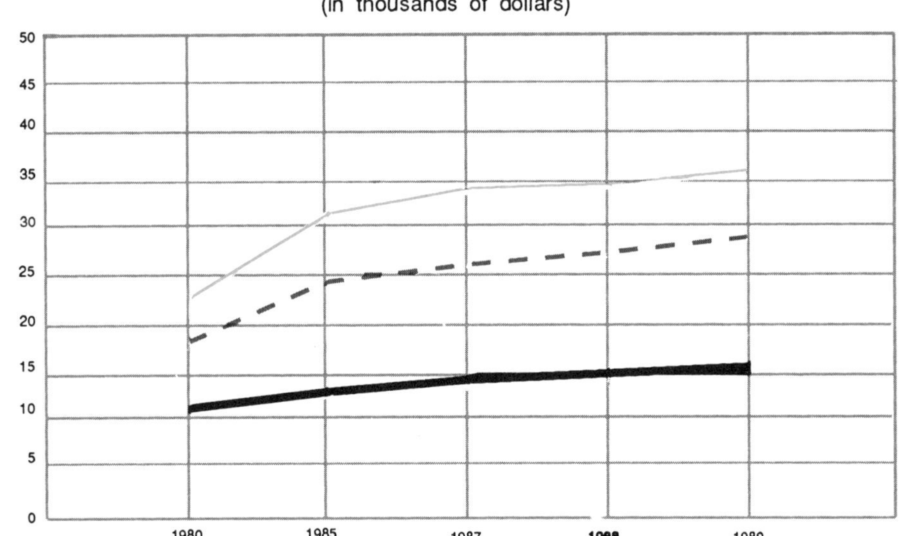

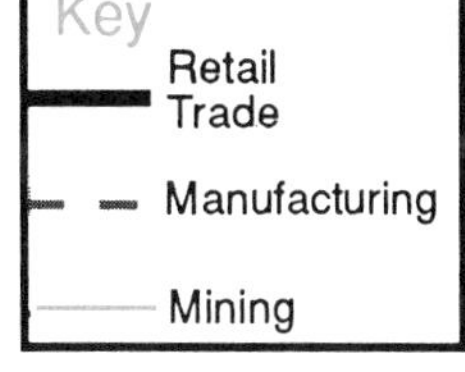

Source: *The World Almanac*, 1992

The relationship between money wages and real wages depends on how fast prices are going up. What happens when prices are going up faster than your wages? You lose ground. Even with more money in your pocket, you are poorer. Your dollar just does not buy what it once did. A general rise in prices—inflation—can wipe out some or all the gains you have made in money wages.

Real wages go up only if the percent of increase in money wages is greater than the rate of inflation.

What are gross pay and net pay? The total wage in a paycheck is called the gross pay (GROHS PAY). Gross pay is usually shown on the left-hand side of a paycheck stub. However, most workers do not receive their gross pay in their paychecks. They receive their **net pay**. Net pay is gross pay minus **deductions** (dih-DUK-shuns). Deductions include such items as taxes. Both federal and state income taxes are taken out of gross pay. So is the payment to Social Security. There may be other deductions, such as payments to pension plans or health insurance. So, while gross pay may be $300, net pay is sure to be closer to $200.

deductions
amounts taken from gross pay for such things as taxes and Social Security

The worker receives less than gross pay. The employer pays more than gross pay. Gross pay of $300 costs the employer closer to $400. Why? First, the employer has to match the worker's payment to Social Security. If the worker pays $45, the employer has to pay another $45. Second, many employers provide sick pay, vacation pay, pension plans and health insurance.

Most employers pay about one-third more than the gross pay of each employee. The added cost includes Social Security taxes and benefits.

Why do wages differ? Not all workers get the same wage. Why do wages differ? Remember that labor is a factor of production. Someone has to pay for it. That someone is the employer. In a sense, the employer buys labor in the marketplace. This means that labor is subject to the forces of supply and demand. When the supply of workers is high, wages will tend to be low. When the supply of workers is low, wages will tend to be high.

What affects labor supply and demand? Many factors affect labor. Some jobs are particularly dirty. Because many people do not want to do "dirty work," the supply of workers for such jobs tends to be low. As a result, people who do the dirty work receive more pay than they might have if the work was "clean." Some jobs are dangerous. Again, many people don't want to risk their lives when they work. Construction workers who work on the top of a skyscraper receive more pay than construction workers who work on the ground.

Dangerous or unpleasant jobs often pay better salaries than safe, pleasant jobs.

Critical Thinking
Name some dangerous jobs that pay well.

Some jobs require that the worker give up something valuable. Many people do not like to work on weekends. Employers often have to pay something extra to hire people who are willing to work on Saturday or Sunday. The same is true for oil drilling on the north coast of Alaska. These oil workers have to leave their family for months at a time. The employer has to make the sacrifice worthwhile by offering high wages.

Skills and talents are the most important factors in determining wages. A doctor, for example, needs many years of costly schooling to learn the necessary skills. The same is true in fields such as the law, science and engineering. People in these professions usually earn high salaries. Other people have special talents. Professional athletes and movie stars often receive huge salaries because they have some special talent.

Education can make a big difference in the level of pay a person receives.

How does discrimination affect labor? Women and nonwhites often face discrimination in the marketplace. Women have made many gains in the past 20 years. Jobs once held only by men have been opened up to women. Still, problems remain. Female workers, on average, continue to earn much less than male workers who do the same jobs.

Women and minorities are often victims of discrimination in the marketplace.

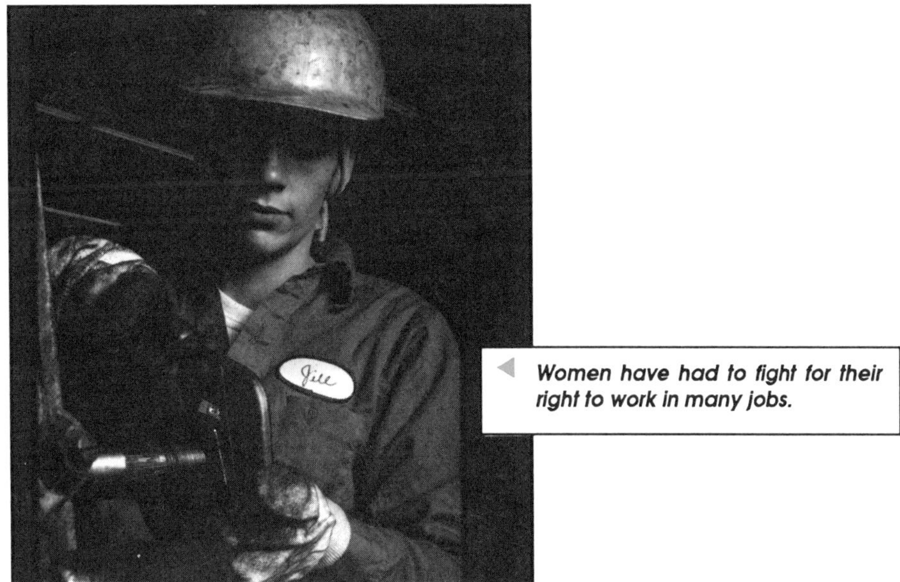

Women have had to fight for their right to work in many jobs.

African Americans and Hispanics face similar problems. They, too, lag far behind white, male workers in terms of wages. Some of the reason is past discrimination. Many African Americans and Hispanics have not been given equal education or job training. As a result, they often do not have the skills required in better jobs. However, this situation is beginning to change.

Critical Thinking
Can a nation afford to keep able people from doing jobs they can be trained for?

Understanding What You Read

1. What are wages-in-kind?
2. What is the difference between regular and overtime wages?
3. Why are money wages different from real wages?
4. Name three deductions that might be taken from gross pay.
5. Give two reasons why some workers are paid more than others.

Workbook Activities

Chapter Test, p. 24
Interpreting a Line Graph, p. 25

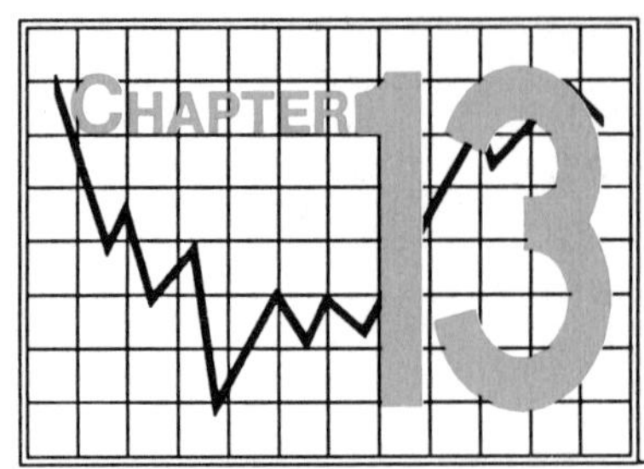

The Distribution of Income and Wealth

The United States is a wealthy country, but not all Americans are wealthy. A walk through any city will prove that there are very rich people and there are very poor people. Why is there such a wide range between wealth and poverty? What can be done about it?

What is income? Income and wealth are not the same thing. Income refers to the flow of money. Income flows in and out of your pocket. The money in your paycheck is income. The money you earn in interest from a bank is also income.

Income is the money you earn. Wealth is the value of what you own.

What is wealth? Your wealth (WELTH) is the value of everything you own. Your music collection, your furniture and your money are wealth. Wealth is a measure of what you own. Income is a measure of what you earn.

Critical Thinking — How could a person with a low income be wealthy?

Not all people who have high incomes are wealthy. Not all wealthy people have high incomes. However, the link between income and wealth is strong. Almost all people with low incomes have little wealth. Almost all people with high incomes are able to gather a good deal of wealth.

How does race affect income? All jobs do not pay the same wages, so all incomes are not equal. Unequal incomes are not based on talent or skills alone. Race discrimination accounts for much inequality.

Figure 1

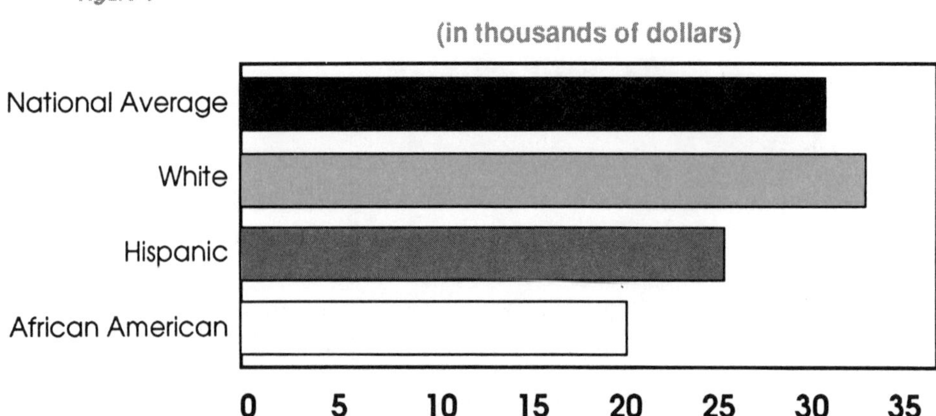

Figure 1 shows that in 1990, the average African American family had a yearly income of $18,676. Hispanic families averaged $22,330. But, white families earned $31,231 a year on average. This gap is not closing.

How does a person's sex affect income? Women, on average, are paid less than men, even when both are doing the same job. Women often leave the work force when they have children, but this does not explain why the wage gap is so large. For example, the average female who is the head of a family earns about half what the average male who is the head of a family earns. This pattern has not changed much in recent years.

Women are often paid less money than men, even when women and men are doing the same jobs.

How does age affect income? Young people earn less than older people. The average head of a family between the ages of 15 and 24 earns less than half what the average head of a family between the ages of 45 and 54 earns. As young workers gain experience, their incomes increase.

Young people who enter the workforce earn less than workers with more experience.

How does geography affect income? Where you live can also affect your income. People in the Northeast and the Far West make more than people in the South. In 1990, the average family in Connecticut earned $41,162. The average family in Mississippi earned just $20,414. One reason for this gap is that Mississippi has many low-paying jobs in farming. Connecticut has far more high-paying jobs in industry.

Geography affects income. People in the Northeast and Far West make more than people in the South.

How does education affect income? Workers with more education make more money. People with high school diplomas make more than those who drop out of school. College graduates earn more than high school graduates. People who hold advanced degrees earn still more. The message is clear: If you want to earn more money, stay in school.

How is income distributed? The distribution of income in the United States is very uneven. Figure 2 divides the country into five parts. Each part represents 20 percent of the nation's families. The bottom 20 percent earned 4.6 percent of the nation's total income in 1987. On the other hand, the top 20 percent of the nation's families earned 43.7 percent of the nation's income in 1987. During the 1980s and early 1990s, the gap between the two groups grew larger.

Critical Thinking
Why does education affect income?

Figure 2

Lowest Fifth	4.6%
Second Fifth	10.6%
Third Fifth	16.5%
Fourth Fifth	23.7%
Highest Fifth	44.6%

The top 20 percent of the nation's families earn almost half of the nation's income.

poverty line
the lowest amount of money a family of four needs to live

What is the poverty line? Figure 3 shows how the income gap affects poverty. Most of the families in the bottom 20 percent fall below the **poverty line.** In 1989 the government defined the poverty line at an income of $12,100 for a family of four. A high percentage of low-income families are either Hispanic or African American. In 1988, about 27 percent of all Hispanic families fell below the poverty line. About 32 percent of all African American families also fell below the poverty line. White families, on the other hand, fared much better. Only about 10 percent of white families were below the poverty line.

Reading a Bar Graph with a Zero Base Line

Some bar graphs have a zero base line. That is, the horizontal line has a value of zero. Think of the zero base line as the zero on an outdoor thermometer. Everything above the zero base line has a positive, or plus (+), value. Everything below the zero base line has a negative, or minus (-), value.

Figure 3

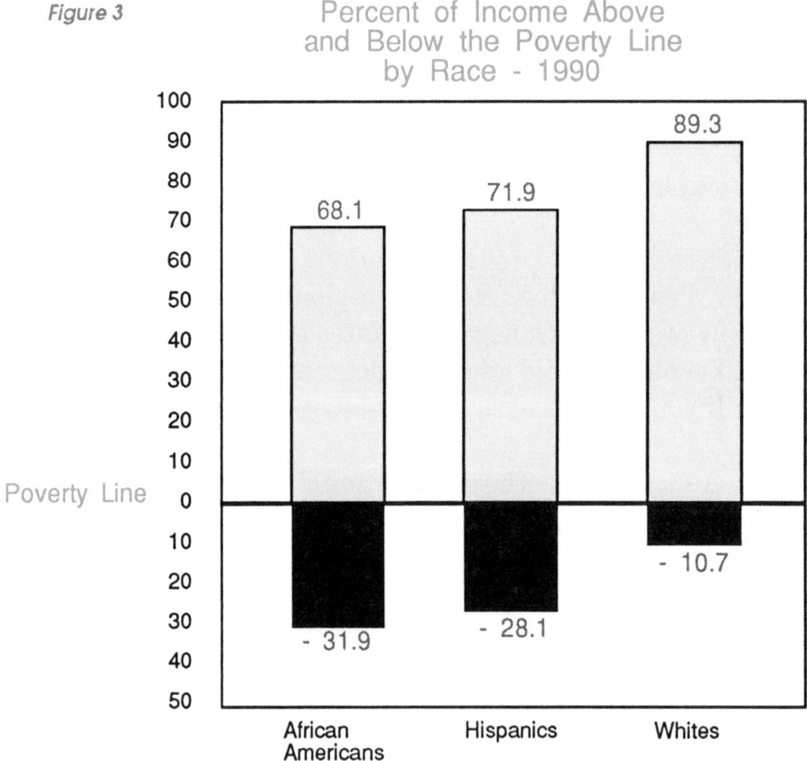

Source: *World Almanac*, 1992

What is the nature of wealth? Again, wealth is not the same thing as income. Wealth includes things such as houses, jewelry, works of art, cars and so forth. Most people take years to gather wealth. Income can vary sharply from year to year. Someone who loses a job loses income. Wealth is different. It usually does not vary much from year to year. A person who is wealthy one year will probably be wealthy the next year.

Critical Thinking
Why does wealth not change much from year to year?

The gap between the incomes of the rich and the poor is great. The gap in wealth is even greater. In the United States, 1 percent of the people own nearly 20 percent of all the wealth. In fact, the top one-half of 1 percent owns 14 percent of the nation's wealth. On the other hand, many poor families have no wealth at all. These families owe more than they own.

Can differences in income be avoided? Some differences in income and wealth cannot be avoided. There is no country on Earth where income and wealth are equal for everyone. Unequal incomes are not the problem. The problem is the huge gap in incomes between the rich and the poor.

Critical Thinking
Would it be a good thing for everyone to have the same wealth and income? Why or why not?

Can education help? Improving the schools, especially in the inner city, can help to close the income gap. Better skills and training would help the children of the poor to get better jobs.

Would a higher minimum wage make a difference? Another way to change the distribution of income is through a higher minimum wage. The minimum wage is determined by law. In 1991, the minimum wage was set at $4.25 an hour. Someone who works all 52 weeks of the year will still earn only $8840. That is well under the poverty line! A much higher minimum wage would guarantee that an adult who is willing to work does not have to live in poverty.

On Your Way Up
Cause and Effect
A *cause* brings about a change in something. The change is called the *effect*. What would the effect be if the tax rates were raised for the rich and lowered for the poor?

What could tax changes do? A third way to change the distribution of income is to change the tax rates. The rates could be raised for the rich and lowered for the poor. Higher incomes would allow poor people to pay for their basic needs without help from the government. This would reduce the need for some expensive programs, such as food stamps and rent supplements.

The distribution of income could be changed by improving education, raising the minimum wage and changing the tax rates on income.

Understanding What You Read

1. What is the difference between income and wealth?
2. How does race affect income?
3. Why does the average family in Connecticut earn more than the average family in Mississippi?
4. What is the poverty line?
5. Name three things that could be done to narrow the gap in incomes between the rich and the poor.

Workbook Activities

Chapter Test, p. 26
Interpreting a Bar Graph, p. 27

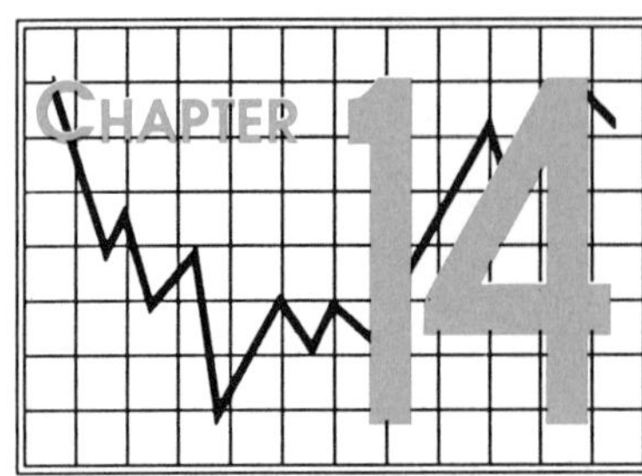

Chapter 14 Labor Unions

labor union
An organization of workers formed to promote the interests of its members

A **labor union** (LAY-bur YOON-yun) is an organization made up of workers. Unions work to promote the interests of their members. Samuel Gompers, founder of the American Federation of Labor (AFL), was once asked what he wanted. His answer was simple. Gompers said, "More." Each year he wanted more for his workers. In other words, Gompers constantly fought for higher pay, shorter hours and better working conditions.

The larger a union, the greater its ability to gain higher wages for union members.

Workers are part of the marketplace. They are sellers. They sell their labor to buyers called employers. Naturally, the workers would like to receive the highest possible wages for their labor. At the same time, the employer would like to pay the lowest possible wages. Workers join unions in order to strengthen their ability to get higher wages. The unions fight for higher wages. The larger the union, the greater the pressure it can bring on the employer for higher wages.

▶ ***Most unions in the 19th Century were not very successful.***

How did labor unions begin? In the 1800s, workers tried to organize unions. They were not very successful. One union after another failed. Some unions tried to do too much for too many workers. The Knights of Labor tried to unionize all workers, skilled and unskilled, black and white, male and female. In the late 1800s, women and African Americans were not easily accepted by the white, male labor force. Also, many skilled workers had their own unions. These skilled workers did not want to be joined with unskilled workers.

Critical Thinking
Would Adam Smith, the founder of capitalism, have approved of labor unions? Explain. See Chapter 6 for help.

What happened to the early unions? The country and most workers were not ready for the Knights. Within a few years, the Knights of Labor lost what popular support it had and collapsed. Other unions failed because they had little money or because they had poor leaders.

Another problem the early unions faced was the fact that the law was against them. People in the nineteenth century strongly believed that each worker was responsible for himself. Each worker was supposed to bargain with the employer on his or her own. The worker had labor to sell. The employer wanted to buy that labor. Human labor, most people thought, was just like sugar or coal or canned fruit. It was to be traded, and its price was to be set by supply and demand.

The employers argued that unions were unfair and un-American. They claimed that unions prevented the free trade of a person's labor for wages. Workers were supposed to bargain as individuals, not as members of a large group. The courts agreed and denied workers the right to organize unions. The workers did not give up. They continued to argue that one poor worker was not a fair match for one rich employer. The only way a worker could force an employer to pay a decent wage was to organize. Only then, with many poor workers acting together, would they have a chance against the rich employer.

Unions allow workers to bargain as equals with employers.

What was the first successful union? The American Federation of Labor, organized in 1886, was the first successful union. It was for skilled workers only. More important to its success, it did not propose what might have been seen as radical, or wild, schemes. Even then, the AFL barely survived. Many of its **strikes** were not successful. Workers on strike refuse to work until their complaints are settled.

strike
a situation in which workers refuse to work until their complaints are settled

During the Great Depression of the 1930s, things changed. In 1935, Congress passed the Wagner Act. This law gave most workers the legal right to organize. If the workers wanted a union, there was nothing the company could do to stop it. The Wagner Act set up the National Labor Relations Board. The board could order elections held in factories so that workers could vote on whether they wanted a union. The Wagner Act also gave the workers the right to bargain as a group. As a result of this law, union membership rose sharply. In 1930, there were only about three million union members. By 1980, that number had risen to nearly twenty million.

The Wagner Act gave most workers the legal right to organize.

What is collective bargaining? Negotiation between union leaders and employers to make a contract is called collective bargaining (kuh-LEK-tiv BAR-gun-ing). When people negotiate, they work together to find agreement on an issue. In labor negotiations, the workers' rate of pay

On Your Way Up
Language Skill
A suffix is an ending added to a word. A new word is formed. Read the words *negotiate* and *negotiation*. What suffix was added to the word *negotiate* to make the word *negotiation*?

is usually the main issue. Fringe benefits are also important. A fringe benefit (FRINJ BEN-uh-fit) is a kind of noncash payment to the worker. These benefits include vacation time, health plans and retirement programs.

Collective bargaining protects workers from unfair treatment.

Collective bargaining is good for both workers and employers. It protects workers from unfair treatment. Collective bargaining helps employers by letting them talk directly to the workers. Many labor contracts contain a no-strike clause. This means that the workers agree not to strike during the term of the contract. The average labor contract runs two or three years.

The Taft-Hartley Act gave the government more control over unions.

What was the Taft-Hartley Act of 1947? Not all the laws passed in recent years have favored the workers. In 1947, for example, Congress passed the Taft-Hartley Act. It was passed because many people thought that unions were becoming too powerful. These people were also upset about the large number of strikes that followed the end of World War II in 1945.

Critical Thinking
Was the closed shop fair to employers? Explain.

The Taft-Hartley Act gave the government more control over unions. The law outlawed the closed shop. A closed shop forced the employer to hire only union members. The Taft-Hartley Act also made it possible for the state to outlaw the union shop. A union shop allowed the employer to hire anyone. However, a new worker would be required to join the union after a certain period of time. Laws against the union shop are called right-to-work laws.

Injunction
a court order not to do something, which is often used to prevent strikes

The Taft-Hartley Act also made it harder for unions to strike, especially if the nation's safety is involved. A steel strike might hurt the country's military defense. In such a case, the President could call for an eighty-day injunction. An **injunction** is a court order to stop something from happening. In other words, the union could not strike for eighty days. After that, the strike could continue. The government, of course, would work hard to negotiate an agreement during the eighty days.

Unpopular strikes have weakened some unions.

How strong are today's union? Unions today are not quite as strong as they once were. There are several reasons for this. Some strikes during the last twenty years have been unpopular. Garbage strikes have left trash on city streets for days. Teacher strikes have made parents unhappy. Bus-driver strikes and air-traffic-controller strikes have made many people angry. Such strikes have led people to feel less sympathy for unions. This has led to fewer strikes. Figure 1 shows how the number of strikes has dropped lately.

Unions are also having trouble attracting new members. Workers today, especially young people, often see the unions as too big and outdated. Shortly after World War II, more than 35 percent of all non-farm workers were union members. Today, that figure is less than 20 percent. Still, with nearly 17 million members, unions remain an important part of American life.

Figure 1

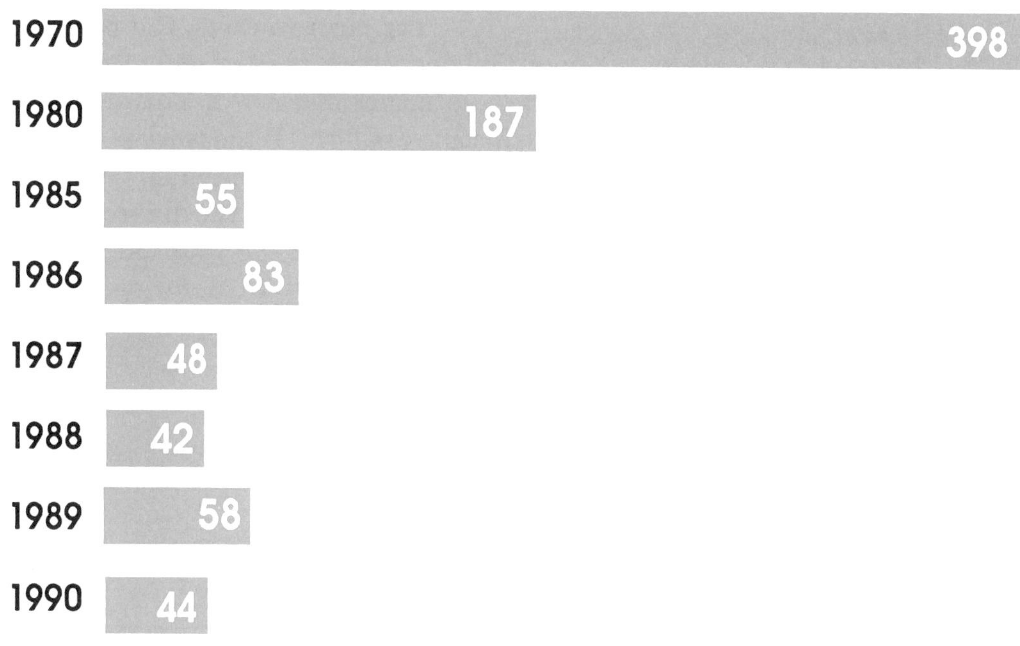

Source: *World Almanac*, 1992

Understanding What You Read

1. What is a labor union?
2. Why were early unions unsuccessful?
3. What did the Wagner Act of 1935 do for unions?
4. What is collective bargaining?
5. What did the Taft-Hartley Act of 1947 do?

Workbook Activities

Chapter Test, p. 28
Making a Line Graph, p. 29

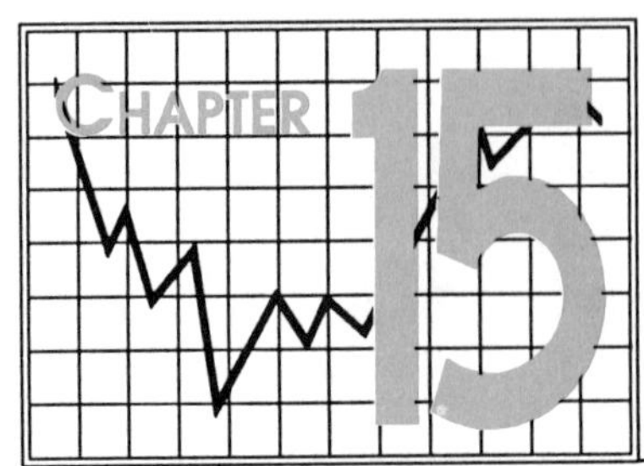

Taxes

Everyone pays taxes. Sometimes the tax is visible. For example, people can see how much the government takes from their paychecks. However, other taxes are invisible. For example, people pay for some things without knowing that a tax is included in the price. Taxes cannot be avoided.

personal income tax
a tax paid on all wages, salaries and other forms of income paid to an individual

What are federal income taxes? For most workers, the **personal income tax** is deducted from their paycheck. At the end of the year, employers send each worker a tax statement, Form W-2. This statement must be filed with the worker's income tax form. If the worker has paid too much tax, the government will send the worker a refund. If the worker has not paid enough tax, the worker will have to pay the difference. The government agency that collects taxes is called the Internal Revenue Service (IRS). More than 40 percent of the money the federal government collects comes from this personal income tax.

Form W-2 Wage and Tax Statement

Form W-2 shows your name, address and Social Security number. Form W-2 also shows the amount of your wages. It tells how much money was withheld for federal, state and Social Security taxes. Form W-2 comes in three parts. One part (Copy B) is filed with your federal income tax form. Another part (Copy 2) is filed with your state income tax form. The third part (Copy C) is kept by you for your personal records.

1 Control number		OMB No. 1545-0008			
2 Employer's name, address, and ZIP code			6 Statutory employee / Deceased / Pension plan / Legal rep. / 942 emp. / Subtotal / Deferred compensation / Void		
			7 Allocated tips	8 Advance EIC payment	
			9 Federal income tax withheld	10 Wages, tips, other compensation	
3 Employer's identification number	4 Employer's state I.D. #		11 Social security tax withheld	12 Social security wages	
5 Employee's social security number			13 Social security tips	14 Medicare wages and tips	
19 Employee's name, adrress, and ZIP code			15 Medicare tax withheld	16 Nonqualified plans	
			17 See Instrs. for Form W-2	18 Other	
20	21		22 Dependent care benefits	23 Benefits included in Box 10	
24 State income tax	25 State wages, tips, etc	26 Name of State	27 Local income tax	28 Local wages, tips, etc.	29 Name of locality

Copy C for Employee
Form W-2 Wage and Tax Statement 1991

Department of the Treasury-Internal Revenue Service

Another source of money is the **corporate income tax**. This is a tax placed on businesses. It brings in only about a third as much money as the personal income tax. Then there is the **Social Security tax**. Sometimes it is called the payroll tax. This is because it is taken directly out of your pay. Remember that your employer matches the amount of this tax you pay. The money raised by this tax is used to give pensions to retired workers.

corporate income tax
a tax placed on business

Social Security tax
a payroll tax taken from your paycheck and paid to retired workers

What are excise taxes and tariffs? The federal government also collects excise taxes. An **excise tax** (EK-syz) is a tax on a certain item. The price of gasoline includes a federal excise tax. So does the price of a pack of cigarettes. Additional money is raised through tariffs (TA-rifs), which are taxes on imported goods. You pay this tax if you buy something that was made in another country. If you buy a Swiss watch, part of the price will be the tariff. The main purpose of tariffs is not to raise money. Tariffs are used to encourage the consumer to buy goods made in the United States.

excise tax
a tax on a certain item, such as gasoline

What are some state taxes? The states have to raise their own money. They do this in much the same way as does the federal government. Most states have both personal and corporate income taxes. These two taxes raise about half the money states need. The other major state tax is the **sales tax**. A sales tax is a tax on the price of goods. The rate varies from state to state. In some states, the rate is as low as 3 percent. In other states, the rate may be as high as 8 or 9 percent.

States often have personal and corporate income taxes as well as sales and excise taxes

In some states, almost everything is subject to the sales tax. Taxes are often placed on such things as clothes, toys, theater tickets and motel rooms. Not every state taxes the same things. Some states do not tax clothing because the tax hurts low-income people too much.

Many states also use the excise tax. Again, this is a tax on a special item. Cigarettes, beer and wine, perfume and cars often have an excise tax. States also raise money by issuing licenses and permits. When you pay for your driver's license, you are paying a tax. If you obtain a fishing or hunting permit, you are paying a tax.

What are some local taxes? Local governments tax property. The **property tax** (PRAHP-ur-tee TAKS) raises about 85 percent of local tax money. City or town officials, called **assessors** (uh-SES-urs), judge what a piece of property is worth. Then they tax it according to its value. The more property you have, the higher your property taxes will be. Local governments also raise a small amount from licenses and permits. A few cities, such as Detroit and New York, even have their own income taxes.

property tax
a tax charged on the value of property

assessor
a person who estimates the value of property for tax purposes

benefits-received tax
a tax paid by those who receive a service or benefit

ability-to-pay tax
a tax that goes up in relation to a person's income

Who should pay taxes? Are taxes fair? Who should pay taxes and how much? These are not easy questions to answer. Should people who get the benefits pay the taxes? This is called a **benefits-received tax** . On the other hand, some people believe that the rich should pay more. This is called an **ability-to-pay tax.**

The gasoline tax is an example of the benefits-received tax. The money raised through gasoline taxes is used to build and repair roads. The person who drives a car many miles pays more in gasoline taxes. The same rule works for highway tolls. If a person never drives on a toll road, he or she never has to pay the toll. Fees to use our national parks are another example. The money raised gives a direct service to the people who pay the tax.

Critical Thinking
Local property taxes support local schools. What does that mean for schools in poorer neighborhoods?

Who should pay for the local fire and police departments? You cannot very well wait until your house is burning down to pay your tax. Clearly, the police should not ask you if you have paid your tax before protecting you. These benefits should extend to everyone, including poor people who may pay little or no property tax. The same rule applies to the national defense. All the people must be protected, regardless of how much tax they pay. In these cases, the benefits-received rule does not work well.

progressive tax
a tax that takes a higher percentage from the rich than from the poor

The ability-to-pay rule says that the people who earn the most money should pay the most taxes. One example is the federal income tax. This is called a **progressive tax** (pruh-GRES-iv TAKS). The more you earn, the more tax you pay. Table 1 shows how this works in theory. At $5,000 income, you pay no tax; at $10,000 income, you pay 5 percent or $500; at $25,000 income, you pay 20 percent or $5,000. At the present time, the federal tax code is less progressive than it once was. There used to be five tax brackets. Now there are only three brackets — 15 percent, 28 percent and 31 percent.

Table 1

Progressive Tax

Income	Tax Rate	Total Tax
$5,000	0%	$0
$10,000	5%	$500
$15,000	10%	$1,500
$20,000	15%	$3,000
$25,000	20%	$5,000

Table 2

Proportional Tax

Income	Tax Rate	Total Tax
$5,000	10%	$500
$10,000	10%	$1,000
$15,000	10%	$1,500
$20,000	10%	$2,000
$25,000	10%	$2,500

Some state income taxes are **proportional** (pruh-POR-shun-ul) rather than progressive. As your income goes up, the percentage of tax you pay stays the same. Table 2 shows how this works. At all levels of income, you pay 10 percent. This means that the poor and the rich both pay 10 percent. If you compare the two tables, you will see why the rich usually support proportional taxes while the poor favor progressive taxes.

proportional
a tax that everyone pays, based on the same percentage

The sales tax is also a proportional tax. Everyone pays the same sales-tax rate. As a result, the sales tax hurts the poor more than the rich because the poor must pay a higher percentage of their incomes in taxes. Poor people often must spend all of their income to survive. They pay the sales tax on all of their income. Rich people can save some of their income and avoid the sales tax on that part of their income.

Sales tax is a proportional tax.

On Your Way Up
Organizing in a Chart
Make a chart with two columns. In the first column, list all the taxes discussed in this chapter. In the second column, describe each tax. Write a heading for each column in your chart.

If tax money is used fairly and wisely, taxes benefit everyone. Taxes build schools and highways. Taxes provide health care and national defense. Taxes give aid to veterans and senior citizens.

Taxes have another important role. They help to close the gap between the rich and the poor. Progressive taxes take money away from the rich and give it to the poor. This is done through the funding of **transfer payments** (TRAN-sfur PAY-ments) or welfare programs, such as Aid to Families with Dependent Children (AFDC) and Food Stamps.

transfer payments
tax money taken from the rich and given to the poor

Understanding What You Read

1. What are federal income taxes?
2. What are excise taxes?
3. Name some state taxes.
4. What taxes do local governments have?
5. What is the difference between progressive and proportional taxes?

Workbook Activities
Chapter Test, p. 30
Reading a Tax Table, p. 31

Mid-term Test, pp. 32-33

Empower Yourself - Cooperative Learning

Look at the chart that you made with the members of your group. Review what you learned about the occupation you researched.

Write a paragraph about the job. Tell whether you are still interested in that occupation. Discuss the amount of time you would have to spend in training for the job. Tell why you think the job is—or is not—worth the effort it would take to prepare for it.

A. On a separate sheet of paper, write the numbers from 1 to 10. Next to each number, write the word in parentheses that makes each sentence correct.

1. The price paid for labor is a (wage/deduction).
2. A (piecework/overtime) wage is based on the number of pieces produced.
3. Salesworkers may be paid a (tax/commission) based on the number of sales made.
4. A (bonus/salary) is a wage paid over the course of a year.
5. A (real wage/bonus) is a special payment based on performance.
6. The plan in which an employer gives the workers a part of the company's profits is called (profit-sharing/wages-in-kind).
7. The amount of goods and services that money wages will actually buy is called (real wages/salary).
8. The gross pay minus deductions is the (real wages/net pay).
9. The amounts taken from gross pay for taxes and Social Security are (commissions/deductions).
10. The value of everything you own is (wealth/income).

B. On a separate sheet of paper, write the definition of each term.

labor union
closed shop
union shop
right-to-work laws
injunction
strike
excise tax
tariff
sales tax
property tax
assessor
benefits-received tax
ability-to-pay tax
progressive tax
proportional tax
percentage

The World of Business

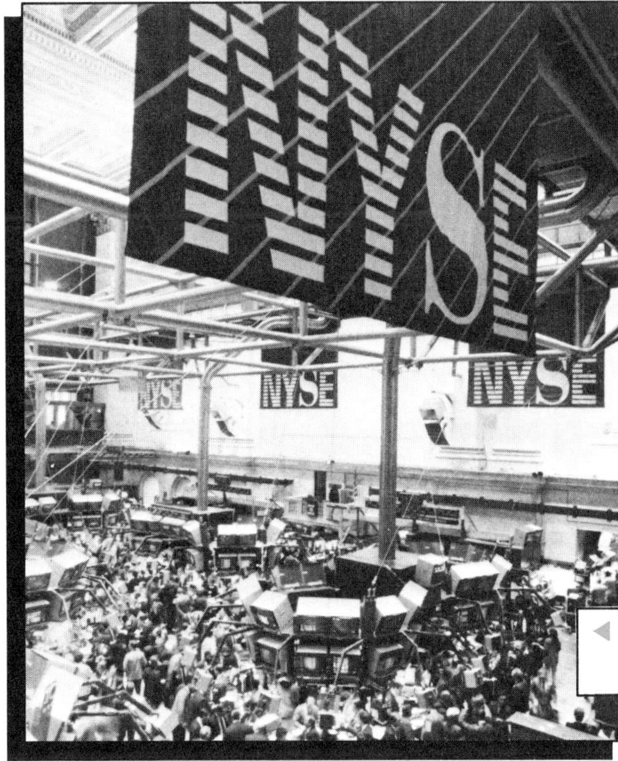

Millions of Americans invest their money in the stock market.

Empower Yourself - Cooperative Learning

You can learn a lot about economics by studying the stock market. Form a group of three to five members. Each group member has $1,000 with which to buy stocks. Choose any stocks you wish from those on the New York Stock Exchange. You can find a listing of these stocks and their prices in a newspaper. The business section of your newspaper may also have articles that will help you choose your stocks.

Invest your $1,000 in the stock market for one month. During the month, you may buy and sell your stocks as often as you wish. If you make money on your stocks, you may invest the money in additional stocks, or keep all your profit and invest only the original $1,000 with which you started your stock purchase.

Keep a record of how you invest your money. Write the date, number of shares and price of each stock you buy. You should also keep a record of the dates, number of shares and prices of stocks you sell. At the end of the month, sell any stocks you still own. Make a chart showing the stocks you bought and sold, and the purchase price and selling price of each. In a column on the right, show how much money you made or lost for each sale. Compare your chart with the charts of the other members in your group. As a group, decide who did best as an investor.

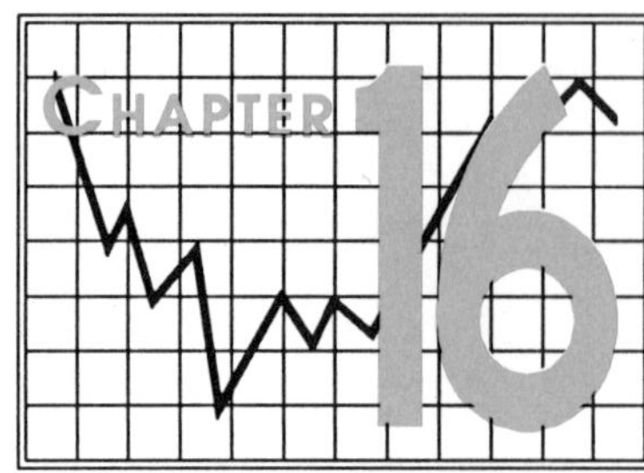

Investments, Corporations and the Stock Market

On Your Way Up
Preview
Before you read this unit, preview each chapter to find out what it will be about. Look for words in **bold** print in the paragraphs and in the margins. Read the questions that begin paragraphs and end each chapter. Look at the photos and illustrations. Read the captions. Predict what you will learn about in each chapter.

An investment (in-VEST-munt) is the purchase of a good or a service in the hope that it will increase in value over time. An investment can take many forms. The key to all investments is faith in the future. Going to school is a kind of investment in your personal future. It is an economic choice you make. You invest your time and effort now so that you might earn more in the future.

▶ ***Getting an education is an investment in the future.***

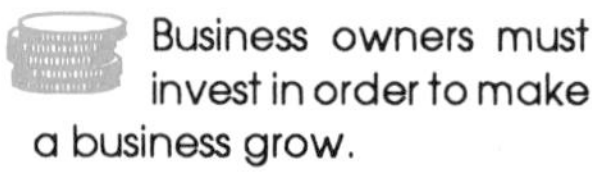
Business owners must invest in order to make a business grow.

Why do owners invest? Business owners must also make investments because businesses must grow. Suppose a business owner named Jose has recently opened the first Mexican restaurant in a suburban town. His menu is a hit. People are willing to stand in line for a half hour just to get a table.

Jose's success has created a problem. His restaurant is too small. There is not enough room for all the potential customers. Jose has two choices. He can keep his restaurant the way it is, or he can expand. If he keeps the restaurant the way it is, other Mexican restaurants will surely open up. If he chooses to expand, he might stay ahead in the Mexican food market. But expansion costs money. Where will Jose get the money?

Investment money can come from profits, bank loans or the sale of shares in the business.

Where does investment money come from? Jose could use his profits to make his business grow. This is a common source of investment money. Owners often put their profits back into the business. Jose can also try to borrow the money from a bank. Such a loan would have to be paid back from future profits.

Jose could also raise money by selling **stocks,** or shares, in his company. People who own stocks or shares are part owners of the company. Jose is the single owner of his restaurant. He takes all the risks, and he takes all the profits. But now he wants to build a much larger restaurant. He is also thinking of opening another restaurant across town. Jose cannot afford to do this by himself. His profits are not large enough. He does not want to borrow all the money he will need, so he forms a corporation.

stock
a share in, or part ownership of, a corporation

Critical Thinking
What are the advantages and disadvantages of owning your own business?

What is a corporation? A **corporation** (kor-puh-RAY-shun) is a form of business ownership. When Jose ran his old restaurant, he was the company. Now he wants to form a corporation, which is like a separate legal person. A corporation has the rights of a real person. Jose's has now become Jose's, Inc. The abbreviation Inc. stands for *incorporated* (in-KOR-puh-rayt-ed), or a legal company. This is an important change. If someone is accidentally injured in Jose's restaurant, who will be sued? It will not be Jose. It will be Jose's, Inc. Now, Jose and Jose's, Inc., are two separate legal "persons." Unlike Jose, Jose's, Inc., has an unlimited life. The corporation can go on even after Jose has died.

corporation
a "legal person" that is owned by the people who hold the stocks

A corporation can buy and sell and sue and be sued.

How is a corporation formed? A corporation is not easy to form because it takes time and money. A lawyer is needed to obtain a charter, or license, from the state. This license divides the company into shares. Each share represents part ownership in the new corporation. An owner who keeps 51 percent of the shares can keep control of the company. The rest of the shares are offered for sale in order to raise the money needed to expand the business.

People who buy shares in Jose's, Inc., hope that Jose's, Inc., will continue to prosper. Success for Jose's, Inc., will benefit all those people who bought shares in the corporation. A shareholder, anyone who holds a share in the corporation, is a part owner in the business. The success of Jose's, Inc., can do two things for its shareholders. First, the corporation can pay dividends to the shareholders. A **dividend** (DIV-uh-dend) is a payment to the shareholders that is based on the corporation's profits. Second, the shares in the corporation can go up in value. The value increases because of supply and demand. There are a limited number of shares. When some people see that Jose's, Inc., is doing well, they will want to buy some of those shares. This increased demand will drive up the price of shares in Jose's, Inc.

dividend
a payment to a stockholder in a corporation

No one knows for sure if Jose's, Inc., will be a success. Even if Jose's, Inc., is a success, no one knows how big a success it will be. The people who buy shares in Jose's, Inc., have a choice. They can hold the shares, or they can sell them. To sell the stocks, the shareholder signs them over to the buyer. Jose has nothing to do with it. Selling and buying shares is quite easy. Every day millions of shares change hands.

stock market
place where stocks are bought and sold

What is the stock market? Most of this buying and selling takes place in a **stock market**. There are several stock markets across the nation. The New York Stock Exchange and the American Stock Exchange are the two major stock markets. These two account for 90 percent of all the buying and selling of shares. This trading is very important. Millions of Americans own shares in different companies. That is one reason why the stock market news is reported every night on TV and in the newspaper.

How to Read a Stock Market Listing

All major newspapers report the trading of stocks every business day. Below you will find a typical stock listing as it appears in a newspaper. A letter has been placed above each column. Each description below explains the information in the column with the same letter. All prices are in dollars.

A		B	C	D	E	F	G	H
52 Week								
High	Low	Stock	Div	100s	High	Low	Close	Change
46	35	CPC Int	2.20	2055	42	41	41	-1/4
33	22	Cabot	.92	100	26	26	26	-1/4
48	35	Car Tec	2.10	78	40	40	40	+1/8
129	63	Celanese	4.40	371	120	120	120	-3

A: The highest and the lowest price per share during the last year.
B: The name of the company or stock. The name is often abbreviated.
C: The most recent annual dividend, or payment, paid per share.
D: The number of shares traded in one day, in hundreds.
E: The highest price paid for the stock during the day.
F: The lowest price paid for the stock during the day.
G: The price at the end of the day.
H: The net change in price from the previous day's closing price.

When the stock market is up, businesses are more likely to invest their money in expanding plants. When the market is down, big companies start to buy smaller companies.

The stock market news lets people know how investors are feeling about the future. If the market is up, more investment is likely. Managers may be more willing to build new plants and research new ways of doing things. If the market is down, managers may think twice before they expand. Something else happens when the market is down. Big companies start to buy up little companies. Instead of expanding their own businesses, they buy the shares of little companies.

The price of stock changes according to the laws of supply and demand.

How does the stock market work? The stock market is like any other market. It is a place where buyers and sellers meet, and the price of shares is set by the laws of supply and demand. In the stock market, however, there is one difference. The actual buyers and sellers do not meet face to face. The stock market floor is not big enough to hold the tens of thousands of buyers and sellers. For this reason, stockbrokers (STAHK-broh-kerz) are licensed to represent the buyers and the sellers. Stockbrokers charge a fee for buying and selling shares for their customers.

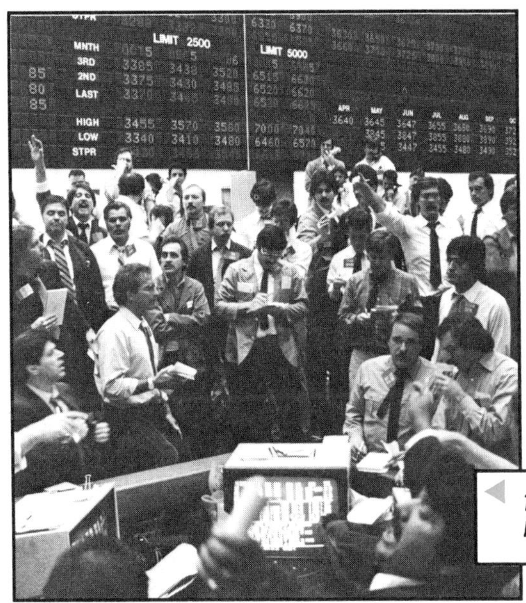

The stock market is a busy place. Stockbrokers buy and sell stocks for their customers.

Why does the market go up and down? The price of stocks is changing all the time. If many people buy stocks in a certain company, the price will go up. If many people sell the stocks of a certain company, the price will drop. No one knows for sure what will happen to the price of a stock in the future.

The selling price of a company's stocks can change from minute to minute. What impact does this have on the day-to-day running of the company? The stock price has almost no effect at all. An auto maker goes on making cars whether its stocks go up or down in price for the day. If the price goes down and stays down, what happens? The company will have a hard time raising money. It will not be able to sell new shares at a good price. This might delay or cancel future investment plans.

The price of a company's stock has no effect on the day-to-day work of a company.

Critical Thinking

Is investing in the stock market a form of gambling? Explain.

Is investing risky? People invest in stocks to make money. They receive dividends on the profits the company has made. When the stocks are up, the company is probably doing well, so stockholders are doing well. However, when the stocks are down, the company is probably not making money. If this lasts for too long, stockholders can lose the money they invested. Investing in stocks is a risky business.

Understanding What You Read

1. What is an investment?
2. What is a corporation?
3. How is a corporation formed?
4. What is a stock market?
5. Why do the prices of stocks rise and fall?

Workbook Activities

Chapter Test, p. 34
Reading a Stock Market Report, p.35

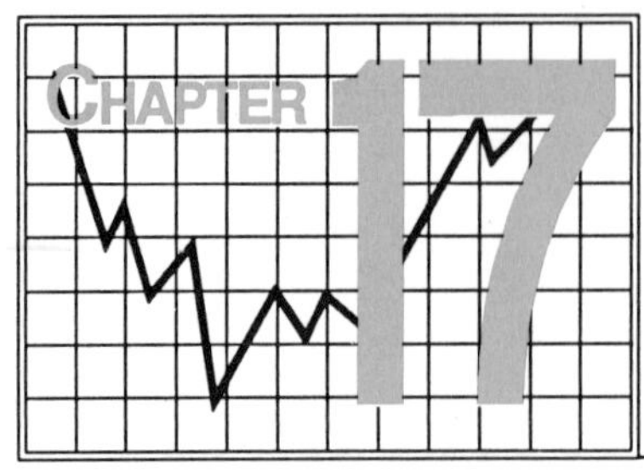

Interest Rates and Banks

Banks will lend money to borrowers who are good credit risks.

Suppose you had $2,000 and you wanted to buy a $4,000 used car. What would you do? You would probably go to a bank to borrow $2,000. The bank would want to know if you are a good credit risk. In other words, would you be able to pay back the loan and the interest charged by the bank. When the bank lends money, a borrower must show that he or she has income, a good record of repaying loans and, sometimes, collateral (kuh-LAT-ur-ul). Collateral is anything of value that a borrower has that can be used to guarantee that the loan will be repaid. Collateral can be in the form of stocks, bonds, real estate or personal possessions.

People must pay interest on the money that they borrow from banks.

Suppose you are a good credit risk. The bank would lend you $2,000. In return, you would promise to pay back the $2,000 plus interest. Interest is the money you must pay when you borrow money from a bank or any other lender. Interest is a percentage of the amount borrowed. The used-car dealer wants all $4,000. The bank's loan makes it possible for you to have $4,000. If you did not have the loan from the bank, you would not have the car.

How does interest work? When you take out a loan to buy a car, you pay interest. When you take out a loan to pay for school, you pay interest. A mortgage (MOR-guj), a long-term loan to buy a house, works the same way.

Failure to pay back a loan results in a bad credit rating.

You should never borrow money unless you are reasonably certain you can pay it back. Two bad things happen when you fail to pay back a loan. First, the bank will repossess, or take back, whatever it is that you bought with the loan. Second, you will have a bad credit rating. You will have a hard time borrowing money in the future because you have a record of not paying back what you borrow.

Critical Thinking

What are the disadvantages of buying everything with cash to avoid paying interest on loans?

There is no such thing as "easy payments." Paying back a loan is never easy. Many families pay 20 percent to 40 percent or more of their income just for interest. On the other hand, most people have to buy some things on credit. Very few people can afford to buy a house or a new car with cash. People often borrow for large purchases. If they waited until they had enough cash, they probably would never own a home or a new car of their own. Credit is needed, but so is a little common sense.

Can interest be earned? You can earn interest. The money you have in a savings account or in a U.S. savings bond earns interest. The bank pays you interest because your money is being used by the bank.

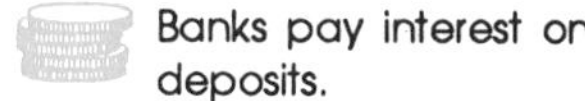

Banks pay interest on deposits.

What is the power of interest? Table 1 shows the power of interest. **Compound interest** does some amazing things to a small amount of money. Suppose you put $100 in the bank and leave it there. See what happens at different interest rates. At 4 percent, it takes nearly 20 years for your money to double. But look at what happens at 8 percent. At this rate, it takes less than ten years for your money to double. At 16 percent, it takes less than five years for your money to double! Now look at what happens after 20 years at 16 percent. Your $100 has become $1,946.08!

compound interest
interest paid on money in a bank and on the interest that the money has earned

Table 1

Interest Table
(compounded yearly)

$100 Deposit	4%	8%	12%	16%
for 1 year	$104.00	$108.00	$112.00	$116.00
5 years	121.67	146.93	176.23	210.03
10 years	148.02	215.89	310.58	441.14
15 years	180.09	317.22	547.36	926.55
20 years	219.11	446.10	964.63	1,946.00

What if you borrowed the $100 at 16 percent interest? After five years, you would have to pay back $210.03. If you waited ten years, you would have to pay back $441.14. And after 20 years, your bill would be $1,946.08!

Most people do not borrow money this way. They pay back a little at a time, which helps to cut down on the effect of compound interest. Still, it is important to be aware of the effect of high interest rates. Knowing about interest rates is very important when you buy a home. Home mortgages can last up to 30 years. Suppose you want a house worth $90,000. Perhaps you would pay $20,000 as a down payment. Then you would take out a mortgage for $70,000 at 10 percent for 30 years. By the time you finished paying off your mortgage, you would have given the bank more than $200,000.

On Your Way Up
Summary
Write a summary, or brief description, of how compound interest is calculated by a bank.

What are fixed and flexible rates? Prices are almost always going up. A dollar this year will not be worth as much next year. This takes some of the sting out of high interest rates. The money you pay back to the bank is not worth quite as much as the money you borrowed in the first place.

fixed interest rate
a mortgage interest rate that does not change even though other interest rates change

In fact, if prices rise very quickly, the banks might lose money. Suppose a bank gave you a mortgage at a **fixed interest rate** (FIKST IN-trist RAYT) of 10 percent. A fixed rate means that the rate cannot be changed. No matter what happens in the economy, you pay 10 percent. Suppose that suddenly prices start going up. Suppose the overall level of prices, or inflation, is at 20 percent a year. Now, even compound interest will not help the bank. It is losing money on your mortgage!

flexible interest rate
a mortgage interest rate that changes with inflation

Banks do not like to lose money, so they came up with the idea of a **flexible interest rate** (FLEKS-ih-bul IN-trist RAYT). A flexible rate can change with inflation. If prices go up, the interest rate goes up. Likewise, if prices go down, the interest rate also goes down. Most banks offer a fixed and a flexible rate for home mortgages.

What do banks do? Banks make money by lending money to people and to businesses. Without this service, people would find it difficult to buy a home and businesses would find it difficult to expand.

Critical Thinking
If you knew that prices would drop sharply in the future, would you want a flexible or a fixed interest rate? Why?

Banks are also a safe place to keep money. Bank deposits are insured and earn interest. The Federal Deposit Insurance Corporation (FDIC) insures bank deposits up to $100,000. If the bank fails, the depositors will get their money back. Banks have safe-deposit boxes where people can store their valuables and important papers. Banks also sell money orders and traveler's checks. When people buy money orders and traveler's checks, they are buying the bank's promise to pay the amount of money shown on the money order or traveler's check. For this reason, money orders and traveler's checks can be used as if they were actual currency.

The Federal Deposit Insurance Corporation insures bank deposits up to $100,000.

People can rent safe deposit boxes from their bank to store their valuables.

What are the types of banks? The United States has many places to keep people's money. The most common place to keep money is the **commercial bank** (kuh-MUR-shul BANK). Commercial banks hold all the nation's checking accounts. These accounts make up three-quarters of the money supply. Commercial banks also have savings accounts. In addition, they provide most of the services other banks provide.

commercial bank
a bank that offers all banking services to consumers

Savings and loan associations are the second largest kind of bank. They are not really banks, however. They are businesses. They accept savings deposits and pay interest. Mutual (MYOO-choo-ul) savings banks are used mostly for savings accounts. Mutual savings banks pay dividends on the accounts because the depositor is a part owner. Credit unions are set up by special such groups as labor unions, churches, or clubs. Credit unions make loans to members on a short-term basis. Their interest rates are often lower than those of commercial banks. As a result, credit unions have become quite popular.

Many people deposit their savings in savings and loan associations, mutual savings banks or credit unions.

How do banks create money? Commercial banks create money. They do this through demand deposits, or checking accounts. Suppose you want to borrow $500 and the bank agrees to the loan. That $500 is put into your checking account. You can spend that $500 simply by writing a check. The government has not printed any more money. Yet, the money supply has grown by $500. Of course, when you pay the loan back, the money supply drops by $500.

Banks create money through demand deposits, or checking accounts.

Banks create money this way every day. But there is a limit. Banks can only lend some of their supply of money. They must keep a certain amount on hand to meet the daily needs of the bank.

Understanding What You Read

1. What is a mortgage?
2. How is interest earned?
3. What is the difference between fixed and flexible interest rates?
4. What are the types of banks?
5. How do banks create money?

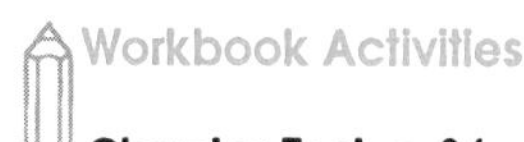

Workbook Activities

Chapter Test, p.36
Reading a Table, p. 37

The Business Cycle

The four phases of a business cycle are: trough, expansion, peak and contraction.

Ever since the United States began, the economy has been growing. But this economic growth has not been steady. There have been some high points and some low points along the way. This up-and-down movement in the economy is know as the business cycle.

Figure 1

The Business Cycle

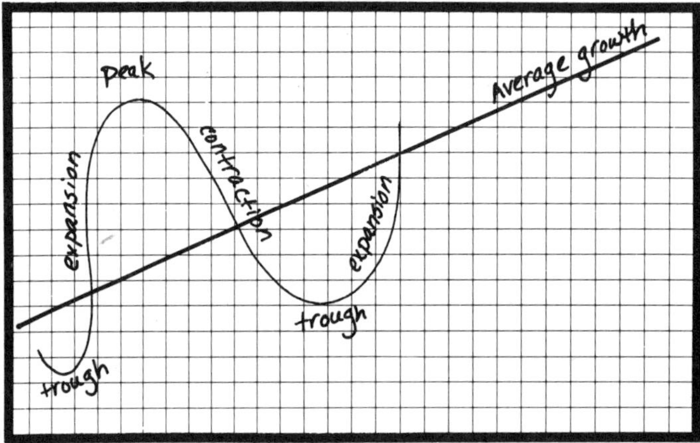

business cycle
the ups and downs of the economy

What are the four phases of the business cycle? Figure 1 shows the basic design of the **business cycle** (BIZ-nis SY-kul). Notice that the cycle has four main parts. No two business cycles are exactly alike. In fact, they are usually quite different. Some cycles last only a short time, while others last much longer. Some cycles even break a few of the so-called laws of the business cycle. There are, however, some qualities that the four parts of the cycle usually contain.

trough
the low point in the business cycle

What is the trough? The **trough** (TRAWF) is the worst period of the cycle. It is a time of low economic activity. Factory production slows down. Factories might produce only half of what they can. Some simply do not run at all. Large numbers of workers are unemployed. Some companies go out of business. Consumer demand is way down because so many people are out of work. Prices also fall. Most companies cannot sell what stock they have on hand. Companies lower prices in the hope that some buyers will be attracted by the bargain. Profits, if there are any, are generally low. Many people feel discouraged about their own prospects

If a trough lasts only a short time, it is a recession. If a trough lasts a long time, it is a depression.

and the future of the economy. If the trough is fairly mild and short-lived, it is called a **recession** (rih-SESH-un). If the trough is very intense and long-lasting, it is called a **depression** (dih-PRESH-un).

recession
a period of lower profits, reduced business activity and high unemployment

depression
a long-lasting trough in the business cycle in which businesses close, profits are very low and unemployment is very high

Sooner or later, something recharges the economy. The government might start a major spending program, such as building interstate highways. There may be sudden increase in investment demand. War always forces the government to spend large amounts of money. The spending fueled by World War II ended the Great Depression of the 1930s. Whatever the cause, the economy begins to improve.

What is the expansion? The next part of the cycle is called the **expansion** (ek-SPAN-shun). Slowly the demand for goods and services goes up. Companies begin to produce more goods and services. In turn, this leads to workers being hired again. More people earning wages means still greater demand. The multiplier effect is now in full swing. Increased spending leads to more investment by businesses. Then the greater demand for goods and services causes prices to go up. But wages are going up faster. New factories are built and others are planned. People now feel good about their prospects and the future of the economy. They are more likely to buy "big-ticket" items such as appliances, furniture, new homes and new cars.

expansion
the point in the business cycle where supply, demand and employment are rising

What is the peak? The period of expansion will, in time, reach its **peak**. At the peak of the business cycle, just about everyone who wants a job can get a job. In fact, labor is in short supply. Companies compete with each other for skilled workers. This sends wages up even faster. Factories are busy. There might even be some shortages of certain goods. Companies cannot keep up with the high demand for goods.

peak
the high point in the business cycle

The peak does not last forever. The level of production starts to fall. The fall in production is often caused by tiredness, poorly skilled workers and rushed work. Companies must face the burden of high labor costs. The cost of scarce raw materials increases. Interest rates have been climbing steadily. All this added pressure puts a squeeze on profits. In time, companies will begin to pull back. Demand and investment begin to drop and output begins to slow down.

> **On Your Way Up**
> **Sequence**
> Words like *then* and *next* are clues to help you follow a sequence, or order. List the parts of the business cycle in order. Write a brief description of each part in your own words.

What is the contraction? The final part of the business cycle is the **contraction** (kun-TRAK-shun). Investment, production and demand all fall off. Confidence in the future begins to sag. People stop buying those "big-ticket" items. Unemployment begins to rise. As a result, consumer demand falls even more. If this trend continues for long, it will lead to a recession or a depression. Then the business cycle will have to begin all over again.

contraction
the point in the business cycle where supply, demand and employment are starting to decline

What is the history of the business cycle? At one time, the business cycle was allowed to run wild. People believed that there was nothing anyone could do about it. This view of the business cycle was held throughout the 1800s and the early 1900s. The depressions of 1837, 1873, 1893, 1907 and 1921 were simply endured. Political leaders felt that there was nothing they could or should do to help the economy. Nature was taking its course.

What was the Great Depression? Then came the Great Depression of the 1930s. President Hoover thought that the depression would last only a few months. In 1930 he said, "We have been passing through one of those great economic storms. . . . I am convinced we have now passed the worst." Hoover was wrong. The Great Depression lasted another ten years. It was the worst depression in the history of the United States.

The depression was so severe that, for the first time, the government took steps to end it. Since the 1930s, the government has taken an active role in trying to control the business cycle.

President Herbert Hoover was wrong about the Great Depression. He said it would not last long. But it lasted ten years.

During the 1980s, the United States enjoyed the longest period of expansion in its history.

During the 1980s, the United States had the longest period of expansion in its history. Consumer demand was at an all-time high. Unemployment was low in most of the country. Inflation was brought under control by the middle of the decade. Energy prices, which had skyrocketed during the 1970s, reversed direction. By the late 1980s, oil and gasoline prices were extremely low. It seemed that the good times might go on forever. Some people even suggested that the business cycle itself had simply disappeared. But the good times did not last forever.

What did the 1990s bring? By 1990 the country was in another recession. Consumer demand dropped off sharply. American automobile makers had a hard time selling cars. Tens of thousands of workers lost their jobs as companies cut back production. The poor people, especially poor children, suffered greatly. For the most part, they had missed out on the good times of the 1980s. In the recession of the early 1990s, things became even worse.

Critical Thinking
Where in the business cycle is the United States today? Explain.

What is the government role in the business cycle? The government tries to control the business cycle. Figure 2 shows the goals of government today. Note what has happened to the peaks and troughs. They have been smoothed out. The highs are not as high as they once were. The lows are not as low at they once were. You can see this when you compare Figure 1 with Figure 2.

The government now tries to control the business cycle to prevent extreme changes in the economy.

Figure 2

The Business Cycle with an Active Government

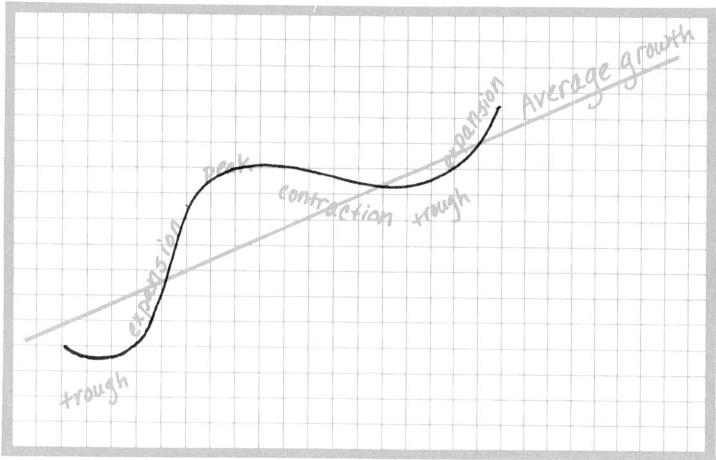

The goal of the government is to make the economy more stable. The government changes its economic policies as the business cycle changes. The federal government can encourage spending in tough times and discourage spending in good times. The aim is to keep the business cycle from getting out of hand.

Critical Thinking
Do you think the United States could ever have another depression as severe as the Great Depression? Why or why not?

Understanding What You Read

1. Describe the parts of the business cycle.
2. What is the difference between a recession and a depression?
3. What happens at the peak of the business cycle?
4. What were the effects of the recession of the 1990s?
5. What does the government do to the economy today that it did not do in 1930?

Workbook Activities

Chapter Test, p. 38
Reading a Graph, p. 39

Look at the chart that your group made to record your buying and selling of stocks. Which stocks were most profitable? Notice how much the selling price of the more expensive stocks changed in value from day to day. Compare these selling prices to those of the less expensive stocks.

Write a paragraph telling what you have learned from your month of investing. Explain whether or not you think that investing in the stock market is a good way to make money.

Review

Complete each sentence with a word from the box. Write your answer on a separate sheet of paper.

mortgage	stockbroker	compound interest	investment
contraction	commercial bank	corporation	recession
credit union	business cycle	stock	stock market
expansion	trough	depression	dividend
incorporated	fixed interest rate	peak	mutual savings bank

1. The purchase of something in the hope it will increase in value in the future is ________.
2. A ________ is a share in a company.
3. A "legal person" that is owned by the people who own the stocks is a ________.
4. The term ________ means "formed into a corporation."
5. Stocks are bought and sold in a ________.
6. A ________ is an agent licensed to buy and sell shares for investors.
7. A long-term loan to buy a house or other high-priced property is a ________.
8. Interest paid on money in a bank and on the interest that the money has earned is ________.
9. A mortgage interest rate that does not change even though other interest rates change is a ________.
10. A ________ is used mostly for savings accounts and pays dividends to the depositor, who is a part owner of the bank.
11. An organization that makes loans to its members on a short-term basis, often at rates than are lower than those at banks, is a ___.
12. The ________ is the ups and downs of the economy.
13. The low point in the business cycle is the ________.
14. The point in the business cycle where supply, demand and unemployment are rising is an ________.

The Role of Government

Keeping the environment safe is every citizens job, but the government has responsibilities too.

Empower Yourself - Cooperative Learning

Managing the nation's resources is every citizen's job. Form a group of five people. Each group member will observe the use of one of five resources—air, water, city land, park land and energy—in your local community.

Keep a journal that lists how your resource is being used and how it is wasted. If you have chosen air, look for sources of pollution. Are local buildings and businesses fouling the air? How? If you have chosen water, look for places where people are polluting rivers, streams and ponds. Examine the use of city land. Are businesses dumping garbage unlawfully? Are the streets littered? Are your local parks clean? What about energy? Look for waste of heat, air conditioning and gasoline.

Meet with the members of your group. Draw a map of your community. On the map, show the places where people are wasting each of the five resources your group studied. Next to each place, write the name of the government agency responsible for the resource.

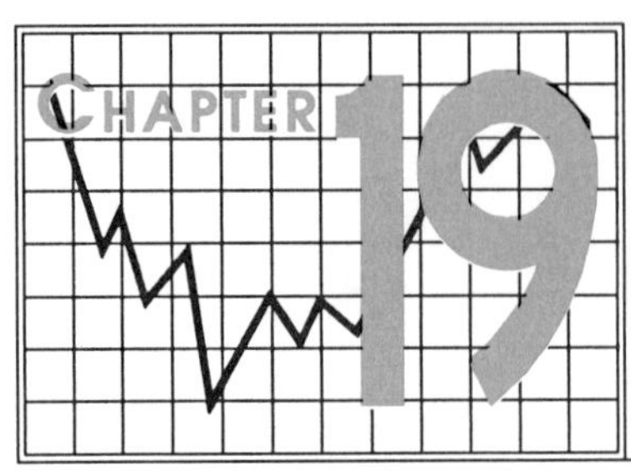

Chapter 19 Monetary Policy

On Your Way Up
Preview
Before you read this unit, preview each chapter to find out what it will be about. Look for words in **bold** print in paragraphs and in the margins. Read the questions that begin paragraphs and end each chapter. Look at the photos and illustrations. Read the captions. Predict what you will learn about in each chapter.

At one time, there was a Bank of the United States. However, many people feared that the federal banking system gave the government too much power. The distrust of the banking system helped to get Andrew Jackson elected as president in 1828. President Jackson refused to extend the charter of the national bank. The bank soon closed.

From that time until the early 1900s, banking in the United States was a very risky business. Whenever the business cycle was in a trough, or low point, banks often had financial problems. Depositors panicked. They took their money out of the banks, and many banks failed.

Federal Reserve System the central bank of the United States, which is run by a board of governors

What is the Federal Reserve System? In 1913, Congress set up the **Federal Reserve** (rih-ZURV) **System**, often called the Fed. The Fed acts as the central bank of the United States. However, the Fed is not a regular commercial bank. The Fed deals only with other banks. For this reason, the Fed is sometimes called the "bankers' bank."

The Fed is run by a board of governors that has seven members. The members are appointed by the President of the United States. Each member serves a term of fourteen years. Members may serve only one term and cannot be reappointed. The appointments are set up so that there is an opening every two years.

Critical Thinking
Should the members of the Federal Reserve Board be elected rather than appointed? Explain.

Alan Greenspan, chairman of the Federal Reserve, is responsible for United States monetary policy.

All national banks must be members of the Federal Reserve System. However, state banks, which are chartered by their states, have a choice. Of the nearly 14,000 commercial banks in the United States, fewer than 6,000 are members. Yet these member banks handle about 85 percent of the banking business in this country.

The Federal Reserve affects the economy. The methods used by the Fed to manage the economy, called **monetary policy** (MON-uh-tair-ee POL-uh-see), help the government to control the business cycle. These methods, or policies, also help to set interest rates. As a result, they affect how much you pay when you buy something on credit.

monetary policy
government control of the business cycle by changing the supply of money and interest rates

What does the Fed do? The Federal Reserve System controls the money supply of the country. Banks create money through loans. The Fed decides how much money the banks can lend. No one wants banks to create endless sums of money. That would ruin the value of all money.

The Federal Reserve System controls the money supply through the use of the reserve requirement, the discount rate and open-market operations.

How does the Fed control the money supply? The Fed controls the money supply in three ways. First, banks are required to keep some reserves of cash with the Federal Reserve System. Suppose a bank has $10 million in deposits. The bank cannot lend out the entire $10 million. If it did, there would be no money left to carry out day-to-day business, such as cashing checks. The bank could not meet withdrawal demands. The cash held by banks to cover such demands is called the **reserve requirement** (rih-KWYR-ment).

reserve requirement
the percentage of a bank's deposits that must be held by the bank or in the Federal Reserve vaults

What are required reserves? The Federal Reserve sets the amount of the reserve requirement for all banks. The Fed might say that 10 percent of all deposits must be kept on reserve. If the bank had deposits of $10 million, the reserve requirement would be $1 million. If the Fed set the level at 20 percent, the bank would have to keep $2 million on reserve. The difference is important. In the one case, there is $9 million available for loans. In the other case, there is only $8 million available for loans.

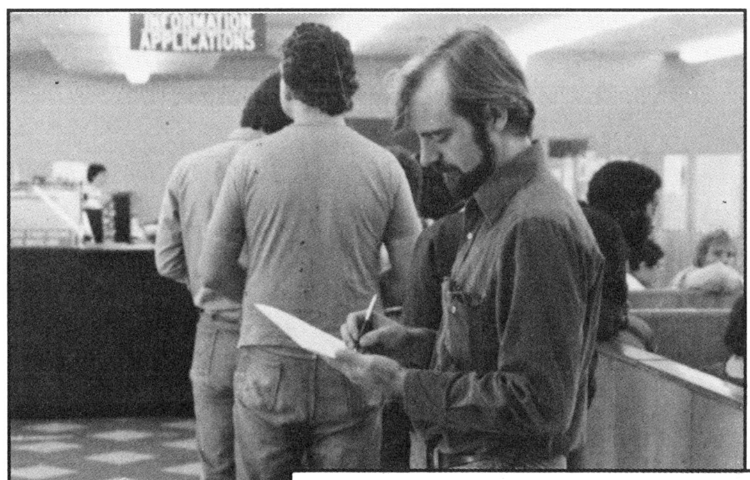

When the Fed lowers the reserve requirements, more money is available for loans.

The Fed's decisions can affect you. If the bank has less money available for loans, the bank may make it harder for you to qualify for a loan. With more money to lend, the bank might ease its lending guidelines.

The rate of growth of the money supply is determined by economic policy.

discount rate
the interest rate the Federal Reserve charges its member banks

What is the discount rate? The second way the Federal Reserve controls the supply of money is through interest rates. The Fed makes loans to banks in the same way that banks make loans to customers. The rate the Fed charges the banks for the loans is called the **discount rate** (DIS-kownt RAYT). When the rate is high, banks have to pay more for their money. They, in turn, charge their customers more. A high discount rate discourages borrowing. Most people and businesses borrow less when interest rates are high. The supply of money goes down. A low discount rate makes loans cheaper. More people are able to borrow money. The supply of money increases. During the recession of the early 1990s, the Fed reduced the discount rate several times in the hopes of sparking a recovery.

open-market operations
the buying and selling of government securities by the Federal Reserve

What are open-market operations? The third way the Federal Reserve can control the supply of money is through **open-market operations**. The money supply is affected whenever the Federal Reserve buys or sells securities. Securities, such as Treasury bills, are similar to stocks or shares. When the Fed buys securities, it uses money from the reserve. By doing this, the Fed puts more money into circulation. When the Fed sells securities, it puts the money from the sale in reserve. That takes money out of circulation. Open-market operations are the most important tools the Fed has to control the supply of money.

Figure 1 shows how the money supply changed between 1980 and 1990. Notice that the money supply grew each year between 1980 and 1989. The rate of growth was determined by monetary policy.

Figure 1

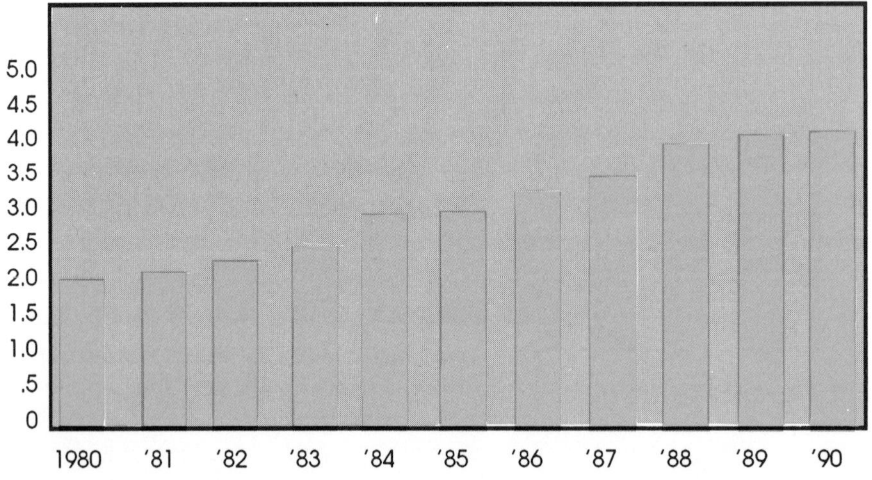

What is the goal of monetary policy? The Federal Reserve System can affect the business cycle. The goal of the Fed's monetary policy is simple. If the business cycle is going in one direction, the monetary policy tries to pull it back the other way. The Fed tries to slow growth in a boom and to encourage growth in a slump. In short, the goal of monetary policy is to flatten out the business cycle. An effective monetary policy prevents large differences between the trough and the peak.

What is a tight-money policy? Suppose the business cycle is going up too fast. There is too much investment and too much consumer spending. If left unchecked, this would lead to an equally rapid fall in investment and consumer spending. The Fed can decide to slow expansion by cutting back on the supply of money. This can be done by raising reserve requirements and the discount rate. The Fed may also decide to sell securities. These steps would lower the supply of money. This policy, which cuts off demand by businesses and individuals, is called a tight-money policy. With tight money, interest rates go up. You may not be able to buy a new car because the monthly payments are too high.

What is a loose-money policy? Suppose that the economy is sagging. Consumer spending is down and so is investment. Unemployment is high. The Fed wants to do something about this slowdown in the economy. It wants to produce more spending. The Fed wants you — and many others — to buy a new car. The Fed wants people to purchase a house or to add an addition to their present home. In order to encourage spending, the Fed moves to increase the supply of money. Reserve requirements are lowered. The discount rate is cut. The government buys securities. This policy, which encourages demand by businesses and individuals, is called a loose-money policy.

The goal of monetary policy is to act as a brake. When the economy is headed for too high a peak, tight money slows it down. When the business cycle is in a trough, loose money gets the economy moving again. A fairly smooth business cycle means stable prices and full employment.

Critical Thinking
Would an economy that was based on pure capitalism have a Federal Reserve System? Why or why not?

On Your Way Up
Cause and Effect
A *cause* brings about a change in something. The change is called the *effect*. What causes a tight money policy? What is the effect of that policy?

The Fed's loose-money policy encourages spending. A tight-money policy cuts off demand.

Understanding What You Read

1. What is the Federal Reserve System?
2. What does the Federal Reserve System do?
3. How does the Fed control the supply of money?
4. What is a reserve requirement?
5. What is the difference between a tight-money policy and a loose-money policy?

Workbook Activities

Chapter Test, p. 40
Critical Thinking, p. 41

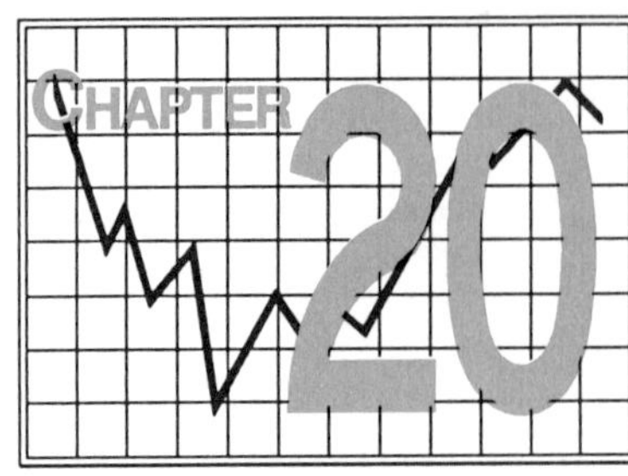

Fiscal Policy

fiscal policy
the government's use of taxes and spending to affect demand

The government uses monetary policy to help control the business cycle. The monetary policy adjusts the money supply. The other means of controlling the business cycle is called **fiscal policy** (FIS-kul POL-uh-see). Fiscal policy changes the tax rate and the spending habits of the government. The goal of both monetary policy and fiscal policy is to change the level of total demand in the economy.

Government spending is necessary to keep the economy strong.

What is government spending? The federal government spends huge sums of money. Figure 1 shows spending of more than one trillion dollars each year. This money is spent for defense, human services and many other things. What would happen if all this spending stopped suddenly? Millions of people would lose their jobs. Thousands of businesses would close their doors. The economy would be dangerously weakened. Government spending is necessary for a healthy economy.

Critical Thinking
How would you be affected if all government spending stopped?

Figure 1

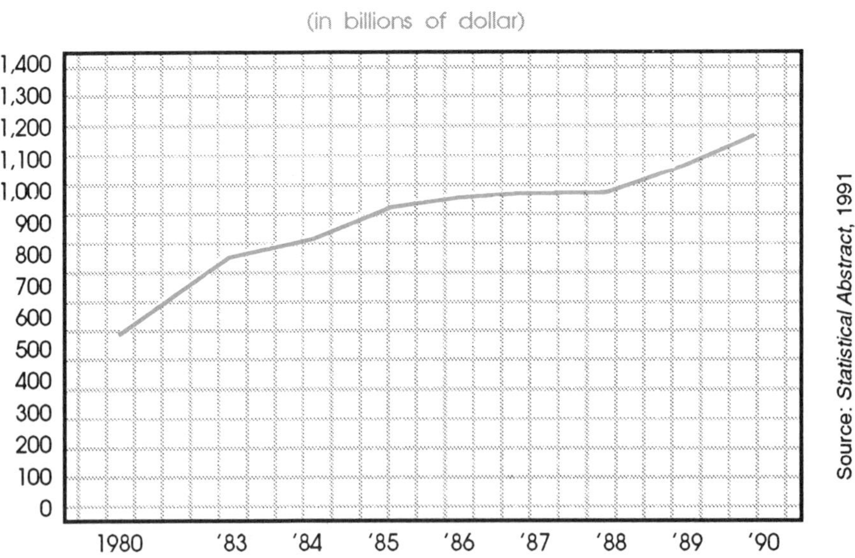

The government uses its spending to control the business cycle.

Not all government spending can be stopped. The government must do certain things. Defending the nation is one example. But there are many possible levels of spending. Spending can be expanded or reduced. In either case, spending has an effect on the economy. The government uses the effect of its spending to flatten out the business cycle.

What was Keynes's idea? Government spending was first used to help the economy during the Great Depression of the 1930s. The Depression lasted so long that people were desperate for a way to end it. They were willing to try something different.

Economist John Maynard Keynes thought the government could "spend its way out of a depression."

An economist named John Maynard Keynes thought the government could "spend its way out of a depression." Since the market economy had no jobs, the government would have to provide them. Congress passed many public-works bills. The government hired people to build roads, plant trees and produce works of art. These projects created demand because the people who worked on the projects once again had money to spend.

Critical Thinking
How do public-works projects create demand?

Government spending can be used to create more spending by the public. Reducing government spending can be used to cut spending by the public. If the economy is doing well, spending programs are often delayed or cancelled.

What is the role of taxes? Government spending is one part of fiscal policy. The other part is taxes. Taxes can be raised or lowered. If taxes are raised, people have less money to spend. When less money is spent, total demand goes down and inflation usually drops. If taxes are lowered, people have more money to spend. Consumer demand increases. Lower taxes also cut unemployment.

The tax system makes the economy more stable because raising and lowering taxes helps to control the money supply.

The government must be flexible. In the early 1960s, Congress cut taxes to fight an economic slump. In the early 1980s, President Reagan persuaded Congress to agree to a 25 percent income tax cut over three years. Both tax cuts helped to create new jobs and higher spending. In 1968, President Johnson asked Congress to raise taxes in order to fight inflation.

On Your Way Up
Reread
Read the last two paragraphs on this page. Write a description in your own words of the role of taxes in the government's fiscal policy.

In 1981, President Reagan said our country was in "the worst economic mess since the Great Depression." His plan, dubbed "Reaganomics," called for lower taxes plus spending cuts.

What is unemployment compensation? Workers who have been laid off from their jobs may receive income called **unemployment compensation** (un-em-PLOY-ment kom-pen-SAY-shun). This income, paid by the government, also helps the economy. The purpose of such a policy is clear. If laid-off workers had no income at all, they and their families would suffer greatly. Consumer spending would drop sharply. A drop in consumer spending can send the whole economy into a recession. When the government helps workers who have lost their jobs, everyone benefits.

unemployment compensation
payments made to unemployed workers that help to maintain consumer demand

Consumers are not concerned with "total consumer demand." They are concerned only with their own demand for goods and services. Someone else has to look at the big picture. That someone is the government. The government changes its spending and taxing policies from time to time. These policies are designed to control the business cycle and to promote the economic health of the nation.

The government uses its spending and taxing policies to control the business cycle and to strengthen the economy.

What is stagflation? Sometimes monetary and fiscal policies do not work very well. The government had a hard time trying to control inflation in the 1970s. A sudden large rise in the price of oil had driven up all prices. The Federal Reserve raised the discount rate, and spending was reduced. Raising the discount rate and reducing government spending should have cut back inflation. The Fed's actions did not control inflation at all. In fact, they caused the worst recession since World War II. People lost their jobs, and the nation had high inflation. High unemployment and high inflation were not supposed to happen at the same time. This strange new condition was called **stagflation** (stag-FLAY-shun). The economy was *stag*nant—not growing—and in*flation* was high.

stagflation
a situation in which there is high unemployment and high inflation

Stagflation came to an end in the early 1980s. Several things happened to bring this about. First, there was a natural upswing in the business cycle from the recession of the late 1970s. This upswing led to greater investment and sales. Second, the government urged Congress to approve huge tax cuts. The tax cuts encouraged further growth. Third, the price of oil came down. People began to feel good about the future of the economy.

What is supply-side economics? Both monetary and fiscal policy try to change demand. **Supply-side economics** tries to change supply. Supply-side economists wanted to change the level of production. They want to increase supply. In 1980, the supply-side economists in the government wanted to lower taxes for businesses and individuals. The supply-side economists claimed that lower taxes would allow businesses to expand production. Businesses could hire more workers. These workers would then have income to spend on goods and services and to pay taxes. Demand would take care of itself.

supply-side economics
an economic theory that relies on tax cuts and deregulation to increase production

Supply-side economists also disliked laws and regulations that hurt production. Supply-side economists opposed minimum-wage laws. They often objected to laws aimed at protecting the environment and public health. Such laws, they said, raised the cost of production. Supply-side economists claimed that such laws prevented the market from working the way it should.

Critical Thinking
Does supply-side economics favor business or the consumer?

Supply-side ideas have caused a great stir among economists. These ideas have been rejected by many. Before George Bush joined the Reagan administration, Bush called supply-side ideas "voodoo economics." Unfortunately, the supply-side policies adopted during the 1980s have led to massive government debt. This huge debt made fighting the recession of the early 1980s much more difficult. The government could not "spend its way" out of the recession because it simply did not have any money to do it.

Supply-side economics led to massive government debt.

Understanding What You Read

1. What is fiscal policy?
2. What would happen if government spending stopped?
3. What was John Maynard Keynes's new idea?
4. What is the role of taxes in the government's fiscal policy?
5. What is stagflation?

Workbook Activities

Chapter Test, p. 42
Making Circle Graphs, p. 43

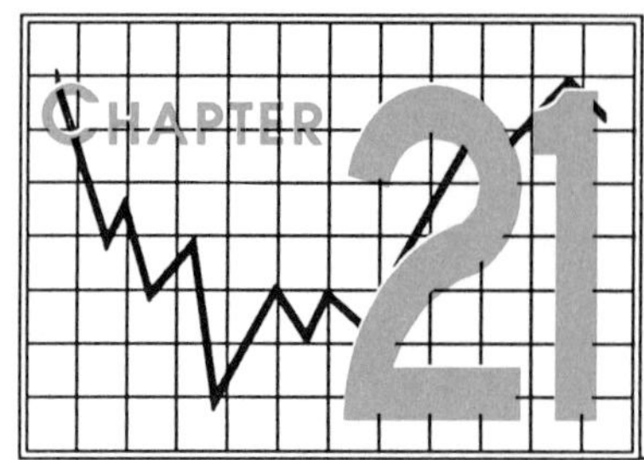

The National Debt

national debt
the amount of money the government owes to individuals and to other nations

Some economists say that the **national debt** (NASH-uh-nul DET) is the nation's number one economic problem. Other economists think that the national debt is nothing to become upset about. After all, they argue, Americans have been in debt since the time of the American Revolution. But there is one thing on which everyone can agree. The present national debt will not disappear any time soon.

On Your Way Up
Using Context Clues
Context clues are words in a sentence or paragraph that can help you understand a new word or idea. What is the meaning of the word *creditor* used in the second paragraph on this page?

What is the national debt? The national debt is the money owed by the government of the United States. Some of the money is owed to governments of other countries. But most of it is owed to American banks, businesses and people like you. When you buy a $50 savings bond, you are really lending money to the government. Your bond makes you one of the government's creditors. A creditor is a person to whom money is owed.

Table 1

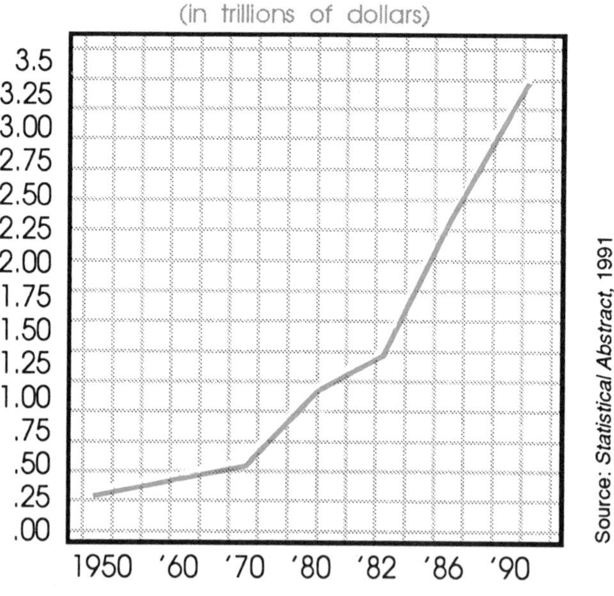

The United States owes its creditors more than $3 trillion.

How much does the government owe its creditors? Table 1 shows how the national debt has grown since 1950. In that year, the debt was $256 billion. By 1960, the figure had grown to $284 billion, and in 1970 the debt was $370 billion. Oil price hikes and inflation affected the economy in the 1970s. By 1980, the national debt rose to $907 billion. Ten years later, the debt had passed $3 trillion!

What exactly is a trillion dollars? It is hard to imagine. When the debt passed the $1 trillion mark, President Ronald Reagan put it this way: "If you had a stack of $1,000 bills in your hand only 4 inches high, you would be a millionaire. A trillion dollars would be a stack of $1,000 bills 67 miles high."

The government must pay interest on its debt.

How have interest payments grown? Like anyone else who borrows money, the government must pay interest. As the debt has grown, so has the amount of interest the government has to pay. Table 2 shows how much interest payments have grown in recent years. About 15 percent of the money the government spends each year goes to pay interest on the debt. That is roughly the same amount of money the government spends on all its domestic programs except Social Security and Medicare. The amount includes what is spent on schools, parks, roads, the environment and health research.

Table 2

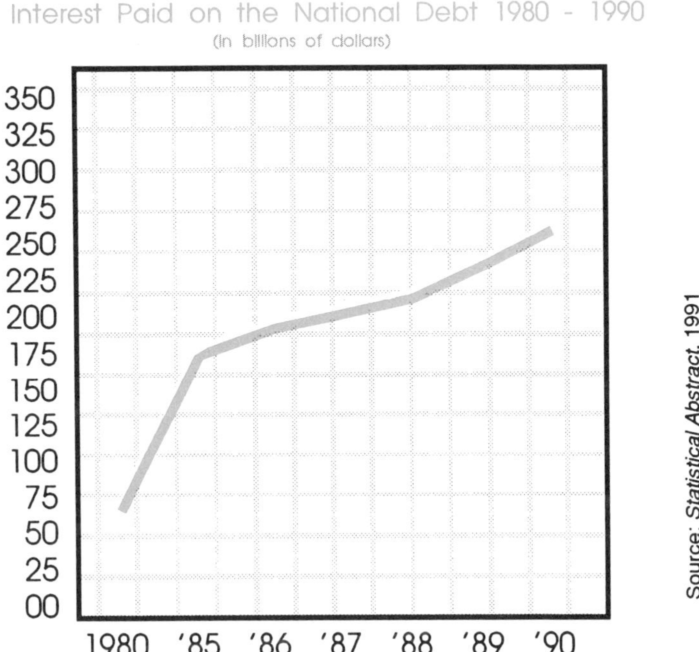

Why is there a national debt? There is a national debt because the government often spends more money than it collects. The result is called a deficit (DEF-uh-sit). The deficit is the amount of money the government needs, but does not have, in order to balance the budget. When the government spends money it knows it does not have, it is called **deficit spending**. Sometimes the government has no choice. Certain bills have to be paid whether the government has the money or not. In some years, the government might have a surplus (SUR-plus). A surplus is any tax revenue that is left over after the government has spent all that it must spend. The last time the federal government had a surplus, however, was in 1969.

deficit spending
the act of spending the money the government knows it does not have

Spending on wars and social programs has increased the debt.

Why are there deficits? The government is often forced to spend more than it collects. Wars cost money, and the United States has fought several wars over the years. In addition, the cost of social programs such as Medicare, Medicaid and food stamps have grown rapidly in recent years.

The government is expected to do much more today than it did fifty or one hundred years ago. For this reason, deficits are common even in peacetime. In 1982, as Table 3 shows, the federal budget was $128 billion in debt. In 1983, it was $208 billion more in debt. Then in 1984, $185 billion more was added to the debt. The next five years showed deficits ranging from $150 billion to $221 billion.

Table 3

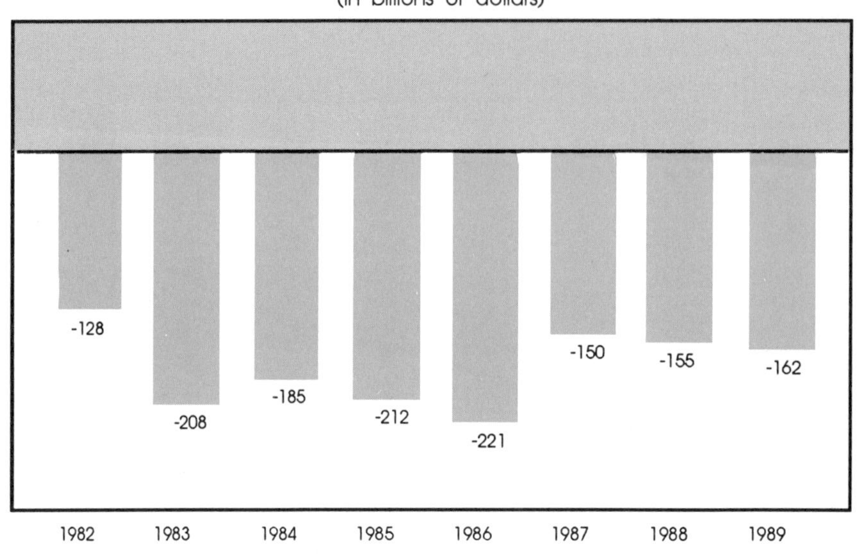

The federal deficit has grown larger and more difficult to control.

The deficit became worse in the early 1990s. The budget deficit in 1991 was $279 billion. The estimated deficit for 1992 was $368 billion! What happened? Sometimes, things happen that no one plans for. In the early 1990s, many savings and loan associations failed. The government had to pay back people who lost their deposits in these failed banks. The final cost promised to be hundreds of billions of dollars. Then there was Operation Desert Storm. Finally, a recession lowered tax receipts and raised government spending on jobless and welfare benefits.

balanced budget
a budget in which income and spending are equal

Is a balanced budget possible? As long as there have been deficits, there have been demands for a **balanced budget** (BAL-unst BUJ-it). A balanced budget would insure that spending is not greater than income. Some people think the federal budget is like a family budget. They say that the government should learn to live "within its means."

Support for a balanced budget was widespread during the 1980s. President Ronald Reagan won the election, in part, on his promise to balance the budget. He also wanted a balanced-budget amendment added to the Constitution. Many states have balanced-budget amendments in their own state constitutions. Reagan failed by a rather wide margin to balance his own budget. By the early 1990s, the balanced-budget-amendment idea had lost much of its public support. The deficits were just too high.

> **Critical Thinking**
> What makes the federal budget different from the average family budget?

What was Reaganomics? Former President Reagan believed in the ideas of supply-side economists. The result was something called **Reaganomics** (ray-guh-NAHM-iks). This was a combination of old economic ideas mixed with supply-side theories and Reagan's own sunny outlook.

Reagan said that everyone would benefit from his program. Deficits would be wiped out, not by higher taxes, but by a growing economy and cuts in spending. The taxes collected from each person would be lower, but many more people would be working and paying taxes. The result, according to Reaganomics, would be more money for the government. Deficits would disappear. That clearly did not happen.

> **On Your Way Up**
> **Fact and Opinion**
> A fact is something that can be proved. An opinion is a belief someone feels. Reagan said that everyone would benefit from his economic program. Was that a fact or an opinion?

Reaganomics also promised to help the poor. The old way of helping the poor was to transfer money from the rich through welfare programs such as Aid to Families with Dependent Children and food stamps. Reagan felt that the poor would be helped more by tax cuts, spending cuts and a growing economy. The economy did grow tremendously during Reagan's term in office. Unfortunately, the poor did not get their fair share of the economic boom. In fact, the poor just grew poorer during the decade.

What is the impact of the national debt? As the deficits grow larger, government services are cut. There is little or no money for new programs, no matter how worthy. Large deficits can also force up interest rates. A government in debt needs to borrow money. When the government competes with individuals and businesses to borrow money, interest rates go up. During the 1980s, the gap between interest rates and the rate of inflation was often about 10 percent. Such a huge gap is not supposed to happen, but it did.

> As the national debt increases, government services are cut and interest rates go up.

> **Critical Thinking**
> Do you think the national debt is a serious problem? Why or why not?

Understanding What You Read

1. What is the national debt?
2. What is a deficit?
3. What is deficit spending?
4. How was Reaganomics supposed to work?
5. How is the United States affected by its huge national debt?

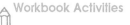

> **Workbook Activities**
> **Chapter Test**, p. 44
> **Making a Line Graph**, p. 45

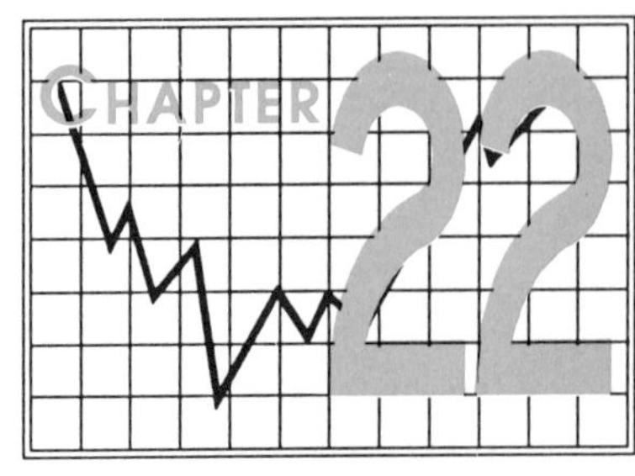

The Gross National Product

Gross National Product (GNP)
the total value, in current dollars, of all goods and services produced in the United States for a given year

You cannot always tell from your own experience whether the economy is strong. Your town or city may not be typical of the nation as a whole. What is needed is a way to measure the whole economy. The **Gross National Product**, or GNP, is such a measure.

On Your Way Up
Main Idea
The main idea of a paragraph is the sentence that tells you what the paragraph is about. The main idea is usually stated in the first or last sentence of a paragraph. Look for the main idea sentence in each paragraph in this chapter. Write each main idea sentence in your notes for use as a study guide.

What is the Gross National Product? The GNP measures the market value of the nation's total yearly output of goods and services. If the economy is strong, the GNP will grow. If the economy is weak, the GNP will grow slowly, if at all. The GNP might even show a drop. During the Great Depression, the GNP dropped every year from 1930 to 1933, which means that the United States produced less and less for four straight years.

The Great Depression, of course, is not typical. Most of the time, the GNP is growing. Figure 1 shows the growth of the GNP since 1980. Notice how sharp the growth line is. In 1980, the GNP was just over $3 trillion. By 1985, it had passed the $4 trillion mark. Despite a recession in the early 1990s, the GNP measured $5.6 trillion in 1991.

Figure 1

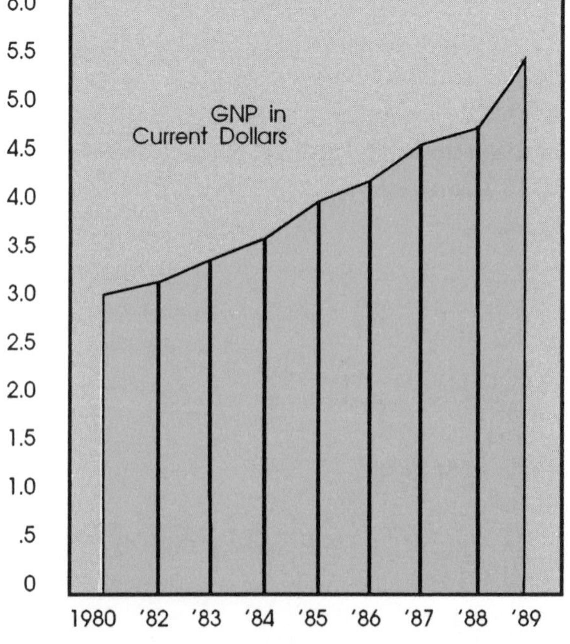

What are intermediate goods? The GNP measures the total output of the nation each year. All services paid for are counted. All final products are counted. Intermediate goods (in-tur-MEE-dee-it GOODZ), however, are not counted. Intermediate goods are goods that are used as part of a finished product. Take paper as an example. It is used to make books. The sale price of each book is counted in the GNP, but the paper is not. The paper's value is included in the price of the book. If the price of the paper and the price of the book were both counted, the value of the paper would be counted twice. A pad of writing paper is a finished product, so its sale price is counted in the GNP.

Intermediate goods, which are used as part of a finished product, are not counted in the GNP.

What items are not counted in the GNP? Some services are also not counted in the GNP. Home-cooked meals are not counted, but a meal at a fast-foods restaurant is. Washing the dishes at home is a service, and so is babysitting for a younger sister or brother. But if no money changes hands, these services are not included in the GNP. The GNP does not count leisure time, even though it has real value.

Some services, such as housework, are not included in the GNP.

The GNP does not measure quality. Some products may be poorly made or they may be wasteful or they may pollute the air and water. If something is sold legally, it counts toward the GNP.

What makes up the GNP? Four major items make up the GNP:

- consumer spending,
- business spending,
- government spending and
- trade with other countries.

By far the most important is consumer spending. Money spent for goods and services makes up about 65 percent of the GNP. How consumers spend their money is important to an economist. Consumer spending tells how well the economy is doing. If times are good, people buy new cars, furniture and maybe a new home. Large sales of such durable goods show that times are good. If sales of durable goods are low, then the economy is sagging. Whether times are good or bad, people will still buy certain nondurable necessities such as food, clothing and fuel. People also pay for services like rent, doctor bills and movie tickets.

Critical Thinking
What happens to the GNP during a slight recession? During a depression?

How important is business spending? Another major part of the GNP is the buying of goods and services by businesses. Businesses also invest in new plants and equipment. These investments create spending through the multiplier effect. Investments also create jobs and increase a business's ability to make more goods in the future. But old plants and equipment wear out. The net national product is the GNP minus worn-out plants and equipment. The net national product is less than the gross national product. On the average, the net national product is about 10 percent less than the GNP.

Business spending includes the buying of goods and services by businesses.

Government spending includes the goods and services bought by all levels of government.

Critical Thinking
Would a cutback in defense spending have an effect on the GNP? Explain.

The value of international trade is added to or subtracted from the GNP, depending on whether the United States has bought more than it has sold from other countries.

current dollars
a measure of the GNP without allowing for inflation

constant dollars
a measure of the GNP allowing for inflation

Is government spending counted? The GNP also counts spending on the goods and services bought by all levels of government. The federal government buys planes, tanks, desks and pencils. The government also buys the services of clerks, soldiers and lawyers. State and local governments also buy goods and services. In the past, government spending has made up about 20 percent of the GNP.

How is international trade counted in the GNP? The last factor making up the GNP is trade with other nations. If the United States sells more than it buys from other countries, the difference is added to the GNP. In those years in which the United States buys more than it sells, the difference must be subtracted from the GNP. In any event, the net impact of this trade on the GNP is quite small. The whole amount rarely goes over two percent or three percent.

What is not shown by the GNP? Look at Figure 1 again. The graph is slightly misleading because it measures the GNP in **current dollars**. Because the graph does not consider the impact of inflation, the real GNP is not shown. To show the real GNP, inflation must be considered. To do this, the GNP must be measured in **constant dollars**. To use constant dollars, you need to pick a year. Any year will do. All other years will be judged based on the dollar's worth for the chosen year. Figure 2 shows the GNP from 1980 to 1989 based on 1982 dollars. Notice how much flatter the line in Figure 2 is than the line in Figure 1. Still, even after inflation has been taken into account, the GNP is rising.

Figure 2

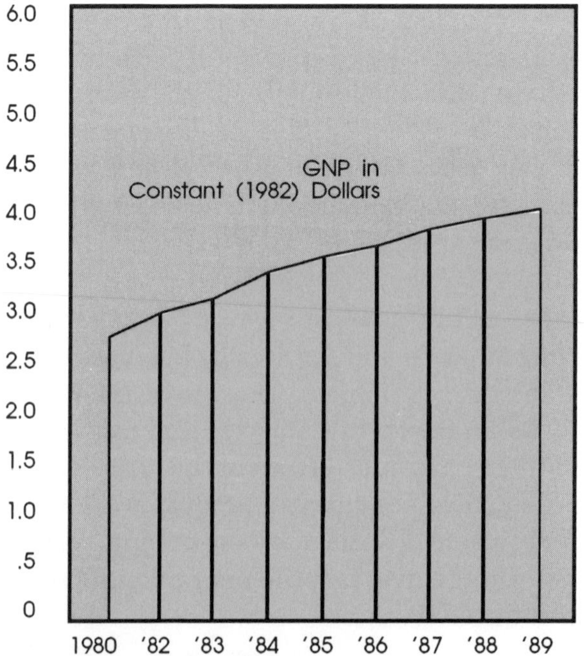

Do population changes affect the GNP? The GNP does not take into account changes in the population (pop-yoo-LAY-shun), the number of people in the country. Assume that the GNP doubled over 20 years. Suppose that during that same period, the population also doubled. The **per capita** (PER KAP-ih-tuh), or per person, growth in the GNP would be zero.

The GNP does not take into account changes in population

What is national income? The national income is the net national income minus indirect business taxes, such as excise and sales taxes. The national income includes income earned by labor, income from rent and income earned by people who own their own businesses. Figure 3 shows how the national income has grown over the years.

On Your Way Up
Organizing in a List
Listing is a good way to remember things. In your notes, list the kinds of income that are included in the national income.

Figure 3

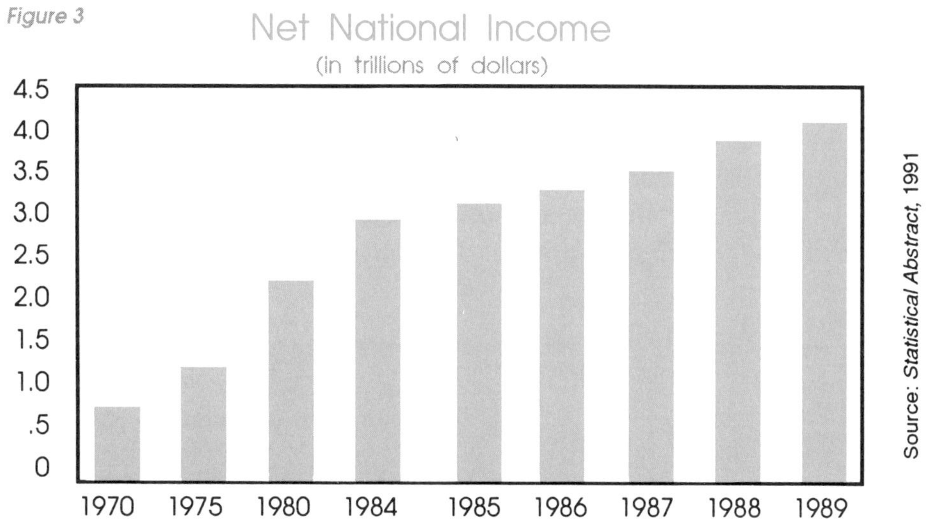

What is personal income? Another measure of the nation's wealth is **personal income**. This is based on what people earn as individuals. Personal income includes all wages and salaries, rent earned, dividends and interest. Personal income also includes transfer payments, such as Social Security benefits and unemployment checks.

personal income
the total amount of money people earn or are given by the government

For most people, however, the most meaningful measure of the economy is **disposable personal income** (dih-SPOHZ-uh-bul PER-sun-ul IN-kum). Disposable personal income tells economists how much money people actually have to either spend or save.

disposable personal income
the total amount of money people have left over after paying all their direct personal taxes

Understanding What You Read

1. What is the Gross National Product?
2. What are intermediate goods?
3. Name three items that are not counted in the GNP.
4. Which four major items make up the GNP?
5. What are the flaws in the GNP?

Workbook Activities
Chapter Test, p. 46
Making a Line Graph, p. 47

Managing Our Resources

The United States is rich in natural resources. The nation has fertile soil, a healthy climate, fine harbors, many rivers and lakes and huge mineral deposits.

Resources can be used to produce goods, or they can be left in their natural state.

How should resources be used? Resources can be used to produce goods, or they can be left in their natural state. A sandy beach or a clean river is as much a resource as a coal mine or an oil field. Not everyone agrees, however, on how these resources should be used. A camper looks at a mountain and thinks about peace and quiet. A real-estate developer looks at the same mountain and thinks about a ski resort and condos. These different viewpoints present a problem.

Who decides whether condos will be built on this farmland?

Resources are limited. A dam built on a river will provide electric power. On the other hand, that same dam may interfere with salmon returning upstream to spawn. Offshore oil wells may make the nation less dependent on foreign oil. These wells may also harm the environment. Businesses want to buy protected wetlands and build plants and factories on them. But wetlands control drinking-water pollution and storm and flood damage.

Critical Thinking
Could selling the federally protected wetlands to businesses end up costing the government more money than the sales bring in?

When is a resource a resource? Whether a resource is really a resource depends on whether people can find a use for it. The oil under the sand in the Middle East was worthless until someone discovered that it could be used as a source of energy. A similar thing happened in United States history. For thousands of years, Native Americans used the plains region west of the Mississippi as their home. They hunted, fished, built homes and raised families. For them, the land was a great resource.

A resource is something for which people can find a use.

In the early 1800s, white settlers passed through the plains region on their way to Oregon. They called the plains region the "Great American Desert." They thought the land was a wasteland on which nothing could be grown. Unhappily for the Native Americans, the white settlers discovered their mistake. By the 1870s and 1880s, many farmers had settled in the region. Using a steel-edged plow and a hardy European strain of wheat, they turned the supposed wasteland into the "Breadbasket of the United States." Today, about 20 percent of the world's wheat is grown there.

Critical Thinking
Why was the white settlers' discovery of how to farm the Great Plains a disaster for the Native Americans?

American farmers once thought of oil as a nuisance. It was so close to the surface that it often oozed out of the ground. Native Americans used it as a medicine. The farmers, however, complained that the oil fouled the local streams and rivers. Then someone found out that the oil could be burned for fuel.

The nuisance had become a resource. Oil was pumped out of the ground and turned into kerosene and gasoline. The kerosene was used in lamps as fuel. The gasoline was just thrown away because there was no known use for it. Then, in 1885, the gasoline engine was invented. Today oil is used for fuel as well as for the many plastic products Americans use.

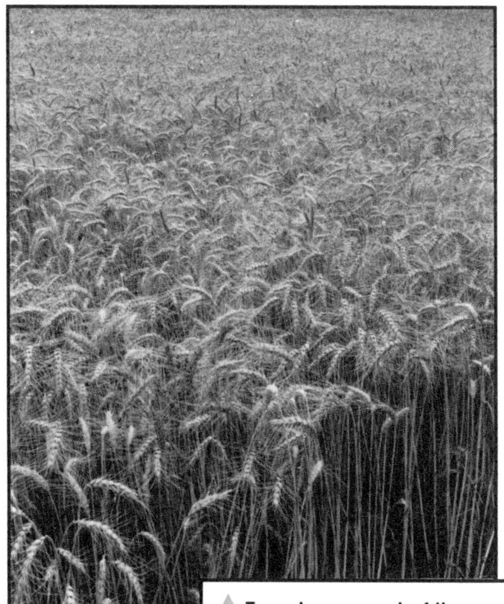

Twenty percent of the world's wheat is grown on the plains of the American Midwest.

Some resources are more limited than others.

In what ways are resources limited? All resources are limited, but some resources are more limited than others. Land is a limited resource. Farms in the United States produce enough food to feed Americans as well as millions of people in other countries. However, the number of farms in the United States is shrinking. Figure 1 shows that there are many fewer farms today than there were fifty years ago. Once the former farmland has been used for factory sites or highways, it is difficult to change the land back into a farm.

Reading a Pictorial Graph

Some graphs use pictures instead of bars, circles or lines. Pictures, or symbols, can make the facts look more dramatic. To understand a pictorial graph, you must understand the key. The key will tell you what each symbol stands for or how much each picture represents. Here is an example:

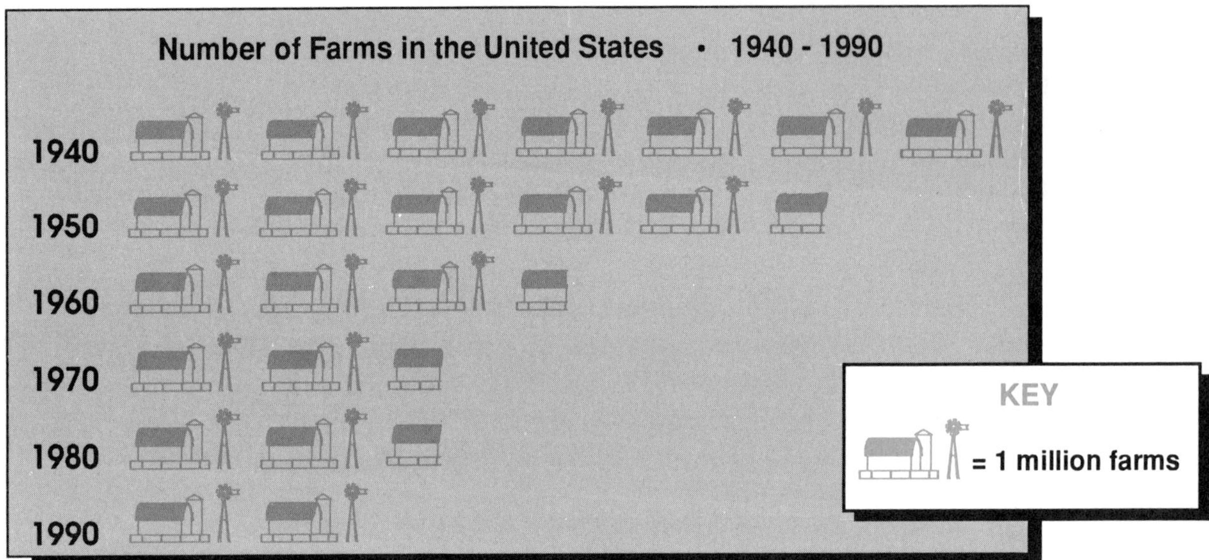

A forest is a resource. There are a limited number of forests in the world, but forests are renewable. Part of a forest can be cut down for lumber. These trees can be replaced by new trees. In this way, trees are farmed like corn or wheat.

The United States depends on nonrenewable resources -- coal, gas and oil -- for 90 percent of its energy needs.

Other resources are not renewable. Oil is a good example. There is a limited amount of oil in the ground. When that oil is used, it cannot be replaced. It is gone forever. Whether the supply lasts 50 years or 250 years depends on how wisely it is used. But sooner or later the oil will be gone. Figure 1 shows that nearly 90 percent of the nation's energy needs come from coal, gas and oil. None of these sources are renewable.

Critical Thinking
What can Americans do to conserve oil and gasoline?

Are there new sources of energy? The long-term hope is to find another source of energy. Solar and wind energy may be part of the answer. More water power would also help. Nuclear power once held much promise, but now it is the center of debate. On March 28, 1979, there was a major accident at Three Mile Island nuclear plant in Pennsylvania. Dangerous radioactive gases escaped into the air. Residents in the area fled their homes, and the plant was closed down.

People's trust in nuclear power was badly shaken by Three Mile Island. But no one had died. Then, in April 1986, there was a major nuclear accident in the Soviet Union's Chernobyl power plant. This time many people died. In recent years, people have been less willing to have nuclear power plants built near their homes.

Recent accidents in nuclear power plants have caused many people to lose their trust in nuclear energy.

Can resources be destroyed? Resources can be destroyed. The air can be fouled by smog as it often is in large cities like Los Angeles. Acid rain damages or destroys rivers, lakes and trees, as well as buildings and monuments. Rivers and lakes can be destroyed by poisonous chemicals. Even the land itself can be made useless. At one time, people thought that resources were endless. Now people are beginning to realize that resources must be saved.

Resources such as air and water can be destroyed by pollution.

Can people have jobs and a clean environment? Many factories produce smoke that contains chemical compounds called oxides. Some of these oxides, when they combine with moisture in the air, form acid rain. The acid rain kills fish in lakes and rivers and stunts the growth of trees. It can even ruin the paint on cars and homes.

Acid rain is not a simple issue. The factories that produce the smoke pollution also produce goods that everyone uses. Closing down the factories would mean doing without these goods or paying a high price for them. Most people will not accept that. If the factories closed, thousands of workers would lose their jobs.

Factories that cause acid rain also produce needed goods.

The other solution is to make the factory smoke cleaner. But that costs a great deal of money. Who should be made to pay? The factory owners? The people in the Midwest? Everyone in the country? There is no easy answer. All sides will probably have to give up some things.

Critical Thinking
Can people afford not to clean up the environment? Explain.

Understanding What You Read

1. What makes something a resource?
2. How did oil become a resource?
3. What new sources of energy could be developed?
4. How can resources be destroyed?
5. How can the problem of acid rain be solved?

Workbook Activities

Chapter Test, p. 48
Making a Pictorial Graph, p. 49

Empower Yourself - Cooperative Learning

Write a letter about the use of the resource you chose for this project. In the case of city or park land, write to the local sanitation department. To report pollution of air and water, you may write to the local office of the Environmental Protection Agency. If you reported to the group about waste of energy, you may write to a local newspaper. Check your local phone book for the addresses.

In your letter, tell what you observed. Make suggestions about how to stop the misuse of the resource.

A. On a separate sheet of paper, write the numbers 1 to 8. Match each term in **Column B** with its description in **Column A**. Write the letter of the correct term next to the number on your paper.

Column A	Column B
1. the central bank of the United States	**a.** open-market operations
2. the interest rate charged by the Fed	**b.** loose money
3. buying and selling of government securities by the Fed	**c.** fiscal policy
	d. stagflation
4. policy that cuts off demand	**e.** supply-side economics
5. policy that encourages demand	**f.** national debt
6. government's use of taxes and spending to affect demand	**g.** discount rate
	h. Federal Reserve System
7. payments made to unemployed workers	**i.** tight money
8. high unemployment plus high inflation	**j.** unemployment compensation

B. On a separate sheet of paper, write the numbers 1 to 5. Next to each number, write the word in parentheses that makes each sentence correct.

1. The percentage of a bank's deposits that must be held by the bank is called the (discount rate/reserve requirement).
2. Promissory notes issued by the government to its creditors are called (supply-side economics/government securities).
3. A budget in which income and spending are equal is called a (balanced budget/family budget).
4. When the government spends money it knows it does not have, it is doing (market operations/deficit spending).
5. The belief that domestic spending cuts and lower taxes will lead to economic growth is called (deficit spending/Reaganomics).

Comparing Economic Systems

People have many different views of how the economic system works.

Empower Yourself - Cooperative Learning

In order to have an economic system, it is necessary to know how the system works—and whether it works. Form a group of five people. Together with the group, make up a list of ten questions for a survey on the United States economic system.

The questions should ask whether people feel the system is fair and whether it works the same for everybody. Ask if people want to make decisions themselves or have someone in the government decide economic matters for them. Ask about issues like national health care and free college educations for everyone. It may be helpful for you to read the unit for ideas while you are making your list of questions.

Each group member should ask at least five people to answer the questions. Be sure to write down the responses accurately. Meet with the group. Prepare an oral or written report on the results of the survey. Each group member should be responsible for reporting the answers to two of the ten questions.

Three Economic Systems

On Your Way Up
Preview
Before you read this unit, preview each chapter to find out what it will be about. Look for words in **bold** print in the paragraphs and in the margins. Read the questions that begin paragraphs and end each chapter. Look at the photos and illustrations. Read the captions. Predict what you will learn about in each chapter.

One basic question in economics is, "Who decides?" Who decides what should be produced? Who decides whether to build steel plants and bridges or whether to make videotape players and designer jeans? Who decides how to combine the factors of production? For example, who decides the right mix of land, labor and capital for growing wheat? Who decides what resources to spend and what resources to conserve? Different nations answer these questions differently. How nations answer the questions depends on the resources they have and the economic systems they adopt.

Every nation in the world has an economic system. No two are exactly alike. Yet there are only three basic ways to run an economy. The three economic systems are:

The three economic systems are the traditional economy, the command economy and the market economy.

- traditional economy — an economic system in which decisions are made according to customs and old beliefs,
- command economy — an economic system under which all the decisions are made by a central power,
- market economy — an economic system based on the working of the marketplace and governed by the laws of supply and demand.

No nation in the world uses one of these systems. Every nation, including the United States, uses a mix of economic systems. Most nations use more of one system than of another.

What is a traditional economy? For most of human history, people have used the traditional economic system. In a traditional economy, things are done the way they have always been done. The basic decisions were made in the distant past. Goods and services are produced according to age-old habits and customs. The amount produced, how it is produced and the right mix of the factors of production are set by ancient practice.

There is little economic growth in a traditional economy.

Does anything change in a traditional economy? In a traditional economy, the son usually does what his father did. The daughter follows th example set by her mother. No one questions the system. No one asks the basic economic questions because the answers are always the same. The system is just there, and the people follow it. There is little or no economic growth in such a system. Every generation does things exactly the same way the previous generation did them. There is no investment in new or more efficient machinery. Any changes that do take place are too small to notice. A great-great-grandchild would feel right at home in the world of the great-great-grandparent.

▲ *The Amish have a traditional economy. They do not use motor-driven plows.*

How does the Amish system work? The Amish people of Pennsylvania have chosen the traditional economy. Their farming methods have not changed much in the past 200 years. They do not use power tools. Their plowing, planting and harvesting are done with horse-drawn plows or by hand. The Amish could, of course, use modern equipment. But they choose to maintain their traditional values and their traditional way of life because of their religious beliefs.

Critical Thinking
What are the advantages and disadvantages of living like the Amish?

The traditional economy clearly has its limits. It is usually used only in a rural economy. The level of production under a traditional economy is limited. Output per worker is low compared to the output of a worker who uses modern machinery. New products and ways of doing things are rarely introduced. Wealth, as measured in material things, does not grow very much or very fast in a traditional economy.

What is a command economy? China, Vietnam, North Korea and Cuba all have command economies. In a command economy, all decisions are made by the government. Until recently, the Soviet Union also had a command economy. Decisions were made by a central planning board called Gosplan. Gosplan was made up of twelve members. The board decided how many toasters or cars would be made in the Soviet Union, not the marketplace. Everyone in the Soviet Union had to follow the decisions made by Gosplan. There was no free choice.

All the basic decisions are made by a few people in the government in a command economy.

The United States economy is a mix of the traditional, the command and the market systems.

Does the United States have a command economy? The United States economy is a mix of all three economic systems. The Amish have a traditional economy. The United States also has some elements of the command economy. The military is set up on the command economy model, and so are public schools. Citizens support public schools through their taxes whether they have children in the school system or not.

The military is an example of the command economy in the U.S.

price and wage controls method used in a command economy to control inflation

Price and wage controls are used in a command economy. In the United States, price and wage controls have been used during wartime or other national crises to control runaway inflation. When the government sets the price of a gallon of gas or freezes salaries at a certain level, it is using the methods of a command economy. The last time price and wage controls were used was in 1971. President Richard Nixon froze wages, rents and most prices for 90 days because inflation was endangering the economy.

Does the United States have a market economy? The economy of the United States is largely a market economy. In a market economy, most people have a share in economic decisions. Producers decide what they want to produce and how much. They also decide how they want to mix the factors of production. Consumers decide what they want to consume and the price they are willing to pay. Retailers, or storeowners, decide what they want to sell and the price they want to charge.

There are no central planners in a market economy. The producers and consumers make decisions for themselves.

The United States economy has millions of decision makers making hundreds of millions of decisions. A market economy has no central planners telling people what to make or buy or sell. The people in a market economy work independently of each other. You can choose to buy—or not to buy—a CD or a new hat. No one is making the decision for you.

What drives a market economy? The consumers and producers in a market economy are driven by self-interest. They are also driven by competition and a desire for profits. A market economy can be unfair and even cruel at times. It creates winners and losers that are not found in traditional and command economies. Market economies have not solved the problem of poverty. But a market economy also offers something not found in the other two systems—economic freedom. Economic freedom works. As a result, the vast majority of the world's nations have adopted economic systems that are largely market economies.

Self-interest drives the consumers and producers in a market economy.

Critical Thinking
Would the military work as efficiently if it were set up as a market economy? Why or why not?

How to Understand Political and Economic Cartoons

Opinions about the economy are sometimes shown in cartoons. These cartoons appear in newspapers and news magazines. Use the tips below to help you understand these cartoons.

- Cartoons do not have to be fair. They are opinions that use pictures and symbols.
- Look for any attempt to make someone look funny or foolish. Rich people, for example, are often drawn very fat.
- Symbols are often used. For example, the dollar sign ($) clearly means money. But inflation can be seen as a monster or as dollar bills flying off with wings.
- When a person is drawn very small, it usually means that he or she is hopeless or ineffective. Watch for unusual changes in size.
- Humor is often used to make a point.
- Be sure to read the words in and under the cartoon.

Understanding What You Read

1. What is a traditional economy?
2. What is the difference between a command economy and a market economy?
3. How did Gosplan work?
4. What elements in the American economy are related to a command economy?
5. In what ways is the American system a market economy?

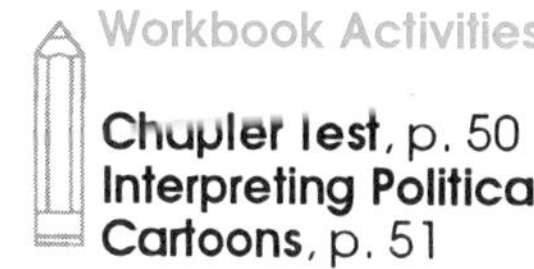

Workbook Activities

Chapter Test, p. 50
Interpreting Political Cartoons, p. 51

Socialism

socialism
an economic system in which all or most of the means of production are owned by the state.

On Your Way Up
Language Skills
A suffix is an ending to a word. When a suffix is added to a word, a new word is formed. The word *socialism* is made by adding *ism* to the word *social.* Whenever *ism* is added to a word, the word becomes the name of a theory, a quality, or an action.

Hundreds of political parties around the world use the word **socialism** (SOH-shul-iz-um) in their name. The Chinese say that their economic system is really socialism. Hitler said that he created a kind of socialism in Germany in the 1940s. The United Kingdom has a system many would call socialism. What is socialism?

What is the difference between political and economic systems?

Political systems are different from economic systems.

Many people confuse politics with economics. The two are closely related, but they are not the same thing. Democracy, for example, is a political system. The United States has a form of democracy that guarantees political freedom. Americans form their own political parties, and they elect their own political leaders. The United States has a capitalist economic system, which is based on economic freedom. Socialism is an economic system, not a political system. The socialist nations of the world may or may not have political freedom.

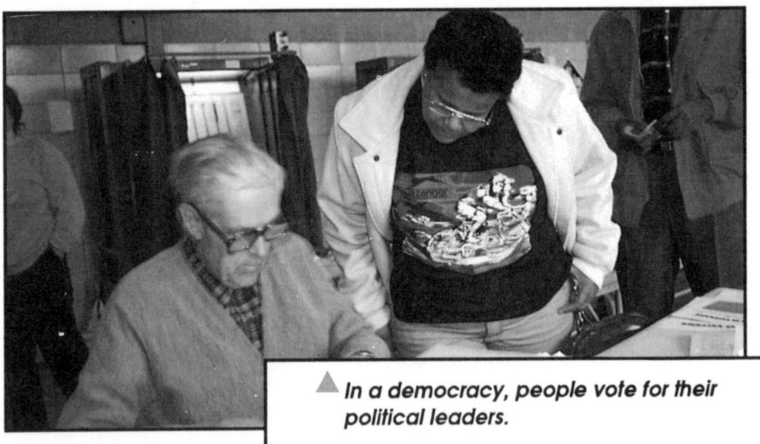

In a democracy, people vote for their political leaders.

Chinese socialism limits personal freedom because the government is a dictatorship.

Since the Chinese revolution in 1949, China has had a form of socialism. However, it has also had a government that is a dictatorship. The government tells its people how to live. Personal freedom is limited, and there is only one party — the Communist party. The Chinese people cannot elect their own political leaders.

The United Kingdom has a form of socialism. The British people, however, never lost their freedom. Their government has been democratic for a very long time. The British people can vote for different political parties. They can also change their form of socialism at any time by voting for a change. Socialism, then, can exist in China and in the United Kingdom. Socialism can exist whether or not there is political freedom.

British socialism exists in a democracy.

What is socialism? Socialism is an economic system in which the factors of production are owned by the government. No two countries have the same kind of socialism. Some have more socialism than others. China has far more socialism than the United Kingdom, and the United Kingdom has far more socialism than the United States.

Critical Thinking
Which is more important, economic equality or economic freedom? Explain.

The government owns and runs all the television stations in the United Kingdom. The government also owns and runs the mines, the airlines and the railroads. In China, the government runs these industries and many more. In the United States, industries are usually run by private companies. As a rule, the more state-run industries a nation has, the more socialist is its economy.

Under socialism in Great Britain, the government runs the railways.

What are the goals of socialism? The big goal of socialism is to close the gap between the rich and the poor. Socialists want to get rid of poverty. They want to achieve the greatest good for the greatest number of people. One of the first steps in achieving socialist goals is to place very high taxes on the rich. This would provide money for the poor. Another step is the **nationalization** (nash-uh-nuh-lih-ZAY-shun) **of industries**. Industries that are nationalized are taken over and run by the state. The state runs the industries in the name of the people. Instead of a few people owning the mines, "everyone" owns them. Money made by the mines does not go to a few people at the top of the company; it is shared by everyone.

The major goal of socialism is to close the gap between the rich and the poor.

nationalization of industries
the taking over of private industry by the government

Steady economic growth is a goal of socialism.

How does socialism achieve growth? Another goal of socialism is steady economic growth. Socialists believe that this can be achieved only through central planning. Every economy needs investment funds to build up the nation's capital goods. Under a market system, the flow of these funds is uncertain. People may choose to invest, or they may choose not to invest. Under socialism, the state can set up a master plan for investment. This market plan, the Socialists believe, will guarantee steady economic growth.

How does socialism use human resources? Under a market system, there is waste because people often try to do the same thing. Ten companies, for example, may be trying to design a safer bumper for cars. They are in competition with each other. Socialist argue that it is wasteful for ten different groups of people to be working on the same problem. These groups have no reason to share their information. Under socialism, just one group of people works on the problem.

Socialists believe that central planning prevents overproduction.

How do socialists avoid overproduction? Socialists believe that central planning prevents overproduction. If too many wheat farmers plant too many acres of wheat, there will be too much wheat. The price of wheat will drop sharply. As a result, some of the farmers might lose their farms. With central planning, only a set amount of wheat is grown. Wheat farmers are told how many acres of wheat to plant.

In the United States, the government restricts the workings of the market in agriculture.

Since the 1930s, the United States government has restricted the free workings of the market in agriculture. American farm policy supports prices for certain farm products, such as milk. If the market price for milk falls below a certain point, the government pays the dairy farmer the difference. The government has also fought overproduction by paying farmers not to produce certain crops.

What is socialism like in Sweden? Sweden is a socialist country. It is also a democratic country. Many people feel that Sweden is a model of socialism that works. There is no hard-core poverty. The average Swede lives life in peace and security. As Table 1 shows, Sweden and the United States compare well with each other.

Table 1

Comparing the United States and Sweden

	United States	Sweden
Life expectancy • female	78.2 years	79.1 years
Life expectancy • male	70.8 years	73.1 years
Infant death rate per 1,000 live births	11.2 deaths	6.8 deaths
Hopital beds per 100,000 population	630 beds	1,496 beds
Doctors per 100,000 population	176 doctors	178 doctors

Source : *The World Almanac*, 1985

What is the Swedish welfare state? Socialism in Sweden aims to provide a comfortable life for all. More than one-third of the national budget is spent on welfare programs. Everyone in Sweden benefits from these programs. For example, everyone in Sweden has free medical and dental care. Prenatal care and child-birth facilities are free, and so are day-care centers. Every family with children under 16 receives a yearly allowance. All Swedish students can attend the state's universities free of charge. Large families receive help with their rent from the state. There is a national pension system.

Unemployment in Sweden is almost unknown. Sweden's economic policy provides everyone with a job. The state runs a job service that moves people to wherever work is available. The job service also retrains workers whose jobs have been replaced by machines.

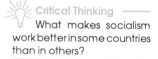

Swedish economic policy provides every citizen with a job.

What are some problems of socialism? The Swedish taxpayer pays for all these benefits. In Sweden, the taxes are very high. Some Swedes think taxes are too high. This has led to strikes by workers demanding higher wages. Taxpayers voted the Social Democratic Party out of office in 1976. The Social Democrats had set up the welfare system.

On the whole, socialism in Sweden has worked. Sweden, however, is not an average country. Its people are well educated, and Sweden is among the richest nations in the world. In addition, Sweden has not fought in any war during this century. It can afford its vast social-welfare programs better than most other nations.

Critical Thinking
Which elements of Swedish socialism would you be willing to pay higher taxes for? Explain.

What is the basic idea of socialism? The basic idea of socialism is central planning. The state answers most of the basic economic questions. The state decides how the country's resources will be used. The state taxes its citizens to fund its programs. In some countries, like Sweden, the process is democratic. If the government leaders do not please the people, they will be voted out of office. In other countries, such as China, there is no choice.

Critical Thinking
What makes socialism work better in some countries than in others?

Understanding What You Read

1. What is socialism?
2. What is the difference between political systems and economic systems?
3. What are the goals of socialism?
4. How do socialists believe economic growth can be achieved?
5. What would socialists do to avoid waste?

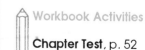

Workbook Activities

Chapter Test, p. 52
Critical Thinking, p. 53

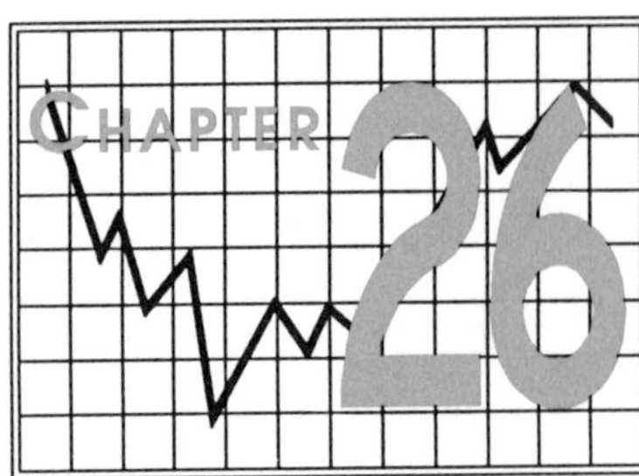

Communism

Communism is a command economy.

Communism (KOM-yoo-niz-um), like socialism, is a command economy. Under communism, the factors of production—land, labor, capital and management—are owned by the state and shared by the nation's people as a whole.

Who was Karl Marx? Karl Marx was the father of communism. He was born in Germany in 1818. Marx was a brilliant student in college, but his strange, new ideas got him into trouble with the government. He was arrested and forced to leave Germany. In 1848, he and his friend Friedrich Engels wrote *The Communist Manifesto*. In the book, Marx and Engels explained their view that the capitalist market system would fail and that communism would take its place.

Karl Marx, the father of communism.

Karl Marx believed that the market system would destroy itself.

What was the "class struggle"? Marx believed that the market system would destroy itself. Under the market system, said Marx, there are only two classes of people—the owners, or capitalists, and the workers. Marx said that the workers are locked in a class struggle against the owners. He wrote that the owners use their power to take advantage of the workers. They pay the workers the lowest possible wage and make them work in unhealthy and unsafe factories. The owners fine the workers for the smallest mistake. Meanwhile, the owners rake in huge profits. The gap between the rich and the poor grows wider and wider with each generation.

Marx believed that sooner or later the workers would rise up and overthrow the owners. After this communist revolution, the workers would control the world, and the market system of capitalism would be replaced by communism.

What was supposed to happen under communism? Under communism, all private property would be abolished, or wiped out. No one would be allowed to own anything, and everyone would be truly equal. There would no longer be an owner class or a worker class. All classes would cease to exist. Under communism, the workers would own all the factors of production. Cooperation would replace competition. There would be no crime, no police and no courts. In fact, there would not even be a government.

Under communism, all private property is abolished.

Where did the communist revolution take place? Marx did not live to see his dream come true. He died in 1883, but he died certain that communism was the wave of the future. He was also certain that the revolution would take place in an advanced industrial country such as Germany. In this, Marx was wrong. In 1917, a communist revolution did take place, but it was in Russia, which was industrially backward. Russia, with the other republics of the Soviet Union, developed into a military superpower. But what happened to the ideas of Karl Marx?

Marx's communist revolution took place in the Soviet Union.

Marx would not have recognized the brand of communism that developed in the Soviet Union. The government did not fade away, as Marx had predicted. The Communist party took over the government. The leaders of the party became the upper class. Party members enjoyed all the privileges of the former owner class. Most of the people in the Soviet Union had a standard of living far below those of capitalist countries.

Critical Thinking
Why have some people in the Third World been attracted to communism?

How did Gosplan work? The Soviet Union never did reach the true communism of Karl Marx. But it did get a command economy in which the state ran just about everything. All the major economic decisions were made by a few people. These decision makers belonged to Gosplan, the central planning agency for the state.

Gosplan set the overall goals for the economy. Every five years it designed a master plan. This plan was then broken down into one-year plans. Detailed instructions were sent to the managers of all plants and factories. These managers told the workers what must be produced. This was a perfect example of a command economy in action. The Soviet economy was run by a series of commands from the top to the bottom.

The system proved to be flawed and quite confusing. It was often slow and full of mistakes. The people in the plants had little freedom. They were not the ones who decided what to produce, and they were not the ones who decided how to produce it. These workers simply followed orders. Each plant or factory had to meet the stated goals given to it by the central planners. If the manager wanted a bonus, the plant had to beat its goal. This often meant that work was rushed and the quality was poor.

The Soviet Union became industrialized because Stalin wanted the nation to be a great military power.

How did the Soviet Union industrialize? Russia was a backward country in 1917. Yet, it managed to become an industrial giant under communism. The Soviet leader Joseph Stalin wanted his nation to be a great military power, equal to the Western nations. He knew that, in order to do this, the Soviet Union needed to develop its heavy industries. Beginning in 1928, the Soviet Union built steel mills, chemical plants and railroads. Five-Year plans set the nation's economic goals and decided how resources were to be used.

How did the Soviet Union treat its consumers? Other industries took a back seat to heavy industry. Simple consumer goods were always in short supply. Consumers had a hard time buying such common items as toasters, blue jeans, soap and toilet paper. Consumers often had to wait in long lines to buy shoes or a sausage. Soda machines did not have bottles, cans or even paper cups. Consumers had to drink their soda from a glass that would be washed for the next person to use.

Collective farms were a failure because farmers had no desires to work efficiently.

How did central planning affect agriculture? Central planning also had a bad effect on Soviet farms. Again, the rigid hand of central planning and a command economy affected output. The Soviets got rid of private farms and replaced them with **collectives** (kuh-LEKT-ivs) and huge state farms. These Soviet farms had their own five-year plans. The goal of Soviet agriculture was to grow all the food the country needed to feed itself. The system never worked. Collective farming was a major failure. As a result, the Soviet Union had to import millions of tons of food from other countries. One reason the Soviet farms did so poorly was that there was nothing in it for the farmers. They received the same rewards whether they worked hard or not. Another problem was that the planners

collectives
large farms created from small, private farms that had been seized by the government and joined together

were in Moscow. They did not know what the local conditions were on each farm. Each farm was told when to plant, how much fertilizer to use and when to harvest. Often these orders were not in the best interests of the individual farms.

On Your Way Up
Summarize
Write a summary, or brief description, of the effect of central planning on Soviet agriculture. Write your description in your own words.

How did Gorbachev change the Soviet Union? In 1985, Mikhail S. Gorbachev became the head of the Soviet Communist party. He knew that something had to be done to reform the Soviet economy. Other Soviet leaders had known about the many failures of the economy, but they never admitted them openly. They also never allowed anyone to criticize government policies. Gorbachev changed that by introducing his policy of *glasnost* (GLAS-nohst), which means *openness* in Russian. For the first time, people were encouraged to criticize poor economic decisions and to identify corruption and inefficiency.

Gorbachev tried to reform the Soviet Communist party.

Later, Gorbachev introduced *perestroika* (per-eh-STROYK-uh), which means *restructuring* in Russian. Gorbachev tried to save communism by making a series of reforms. State-owned companies were told to earn a profit or close their doors. Prices that were once set by the government could be negotiated between buyer and seller. The government was told to cut back on central planning. The government even encouraged private enterprise to produce many consumer goods and services.

What did Gorbachev accomplish? Gorbachev's reforms led to results that no one could have foreseen in 1985. By the beginning of the 1990s, the Soviet Union lost its control of the communist countries of Eastern Europe. Countries such as Poland, Czechoslovakia and East Germany overthrew their communist leaders and traditions. One by one the Eastern European states accepted democratic freedoms and a market economy.

In 1992, the former Soviet Union began to change to a market-based economy.

An attempt by conservative communists to overthrow Gorbachev failed. A new leader, Boris Yeltsin, outlawed the Communist party in Russia. Soon the party was finished in all the Soviet republics, and the Soviet Union fell apart. A new union of the republics, called the Commonwealth of Independent States, was formed. In 1992, the republics of the new commonwealth struggled to change to a market-based economy.

Critical Thinking
Why do you think the Commonwealth of Independent States is having difficulty changing to a market economy?

Understanding What You Read

1. What is communism?
2. What did Marx believe about the class struggle?
3. How did Soviet communism run its command economy?
4. What happened to consumers under Soviet communism?
5. What problems did Soviet farmers have because of central planning?

Workbook Activities

Chapter Test, p. 54
Critical Thinking, p. 55

Empower Yourself - Cooperative Learning

After you have reported on the results of your survey, write a paragraph about what the experience has taught you. Discuss whether the people you talked to understood the advantages and disadvantages of a market economy. Did some of the people want a different system? What might have been their reasons for preferring another system?

Explain which economic system you yourself prefer. Give reasons for your choice.

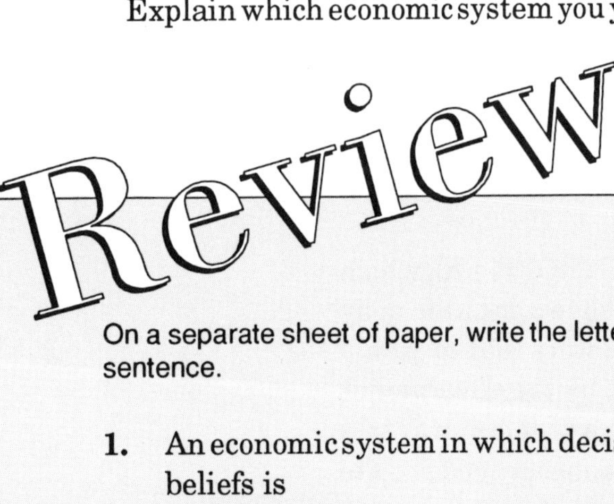

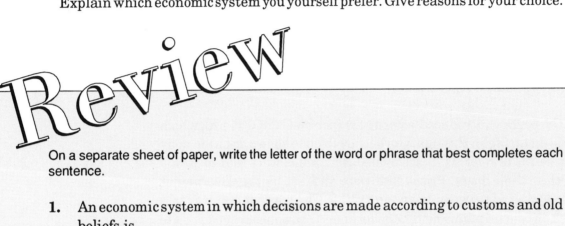

On a separate sheet of paper, write the letter of the word or phrase that best completes each sentence.

1. An economic system in which decisions are made according to customs and old beliefs is
a. traditional b. command c. market economy

2. The central planning authority in the former Soviet Union was a
a. C-Span b. the Marshall Plan c. Gosplan

3. Price and wage controls are used to control
a. taxes b. inflation c. people

4. Under socialism, all or most of the means of production are owned by
a. the state b. businesses c. the wealthy

5. The taking over of private industry by the government is
a. illegal b. democracy c. nationalization

6. The economies of China, Vietnam, North Korea and Cuba are
a. command b. market c. traditional

7. For the most part, the United States economy is
a. traditional b. market c. command

8. One example of command economy in the United States is
a. the military b. the stock market c. discount stores

9. A market economy has no
a. decision makers b. central planning c. consumers

10. Consumers and producers in a market economy are driven by self-interest, competition and the desire for
a. luxury b. independence c. profits

11. Sweden is an example of a country with a system that is
a. socialist b. communist c. undemocratic

12. The "father of communism" was
a. Joseph Stalin b. Mikhail Gorbachev c. Karl Marx

A World View

When you buy a product, do you check to see where it was made?

Empower Yourself - Cooperative Learning

People often buy products without paying much attention to where the products were made. Form a group of four or five people. Each member of the group will choose two items from this list of ten products: shoes, perfume, cars, CD players, chocolates, cookware, china dishes, rugs, computers, calculators.

Go to a store that sells the products you have chosen to research. Find two similar examples of each product, one made in the United States and the other made in a foreign country. Compare the two products. Write down the price of each product and your opinion of its quality.

Meet with the group to create a chart. Across the top of the chart, put the following headings: PRODUCT, PRICE, QUALITY, AMERICAN-MADE, IMPORTED. Fill in the chart with the information your group has gathered. For each item, indicate whether you would buy the American-made or the imported product.

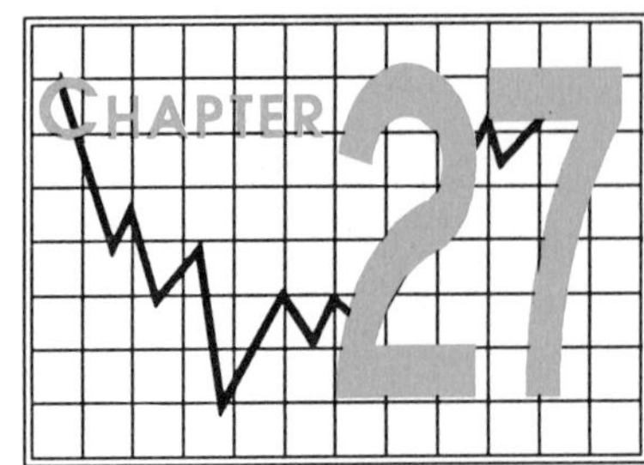

World Trade

On Your Way Up
Preview
Before you read this unit, preview each chapter to find out what it will be about. Look for words in **bold** print in the paragraphs and in the margins. Read the questions that begin paragraphs and end each chapter. Look at the photos and illustrations. Read the captions. Predict what you will learn about in each chapter.

Think of how different your life would be if there was no world trade. What would happen if all the countries of the world stopped trading with each other? For one thing, you would not have any coffee, tea or hot chocolate to drink. You would not have bananas or grapes to eat in the winter. Your choice of what bicycle to own would be greatly limited. Even your telephone service would be different.

The United States is very rich in natural resources. However, no nation is so rich that it does not need the goods and services other countries can provide.

Why is trade necessary? What would happen if there was no trade between the states? Kansas, for example, would have to make all its own goods, and so would all the other states. How much poorer would American consumers be in terms of the quality of their lives? They would be much poorer! The people in Texas would never taste a crisp McIntosh apple. The people in Hawaii would have to make their own minivans. Only students from New York would get to see the Statue of Liberty.

Americans need each other. They need New England to grow its great McIntosh apples. They need Michigan to make minivans. Students from other parts of the United States should be able to take field trips to New York City. The United States would be much poorer without trade between the states.

World trade is necessary because the world's resources are not evenly divided.

How are resources shared? The nations of the world need each other in the same way that the states depend on each other. World trade helps all nations. Trade is critical because the world's resources are not evenly divided. Some countries, such as South Africa and Brazil, are rich in resources. Other countries, such as Chad in central Africa, are poor in resources.

Which minerals are imported by the United States? The United States is not rich in some minerals. South Africa has 82 percent of the world's reserves of platinum. The United States has less than 0.1 percent. Some small nations have large reserves of important minerals. New

Caledonia is a Pacific island barely the size of Connecticut. Yet it has 19 percent of the world's cobalt. The United States has almost none. Gabon, a small African country, has more manganese than the United States. The United States must trade to get these minerals. Such trade makes the nation stronger. Without this trade, the United States would not be able to manufacture many of its products.

The United States depends on other countries for its supplies of such minerals as platinum, colbalt and manganese.

Table 1 shows how much the United States relies on foreign countries for its source of vital minerals. For example, the United States imports 100 percent of its manganese, which is used in steelmaking. The United States imports 97 percent of the bauxite and alumina that it uses to make aluminum. The nation also imports 73 percent of the tungsten used in making lightbulbs. The same pattern of dependence is true with many other important minerals, as Table 1 indicates.

Table 1

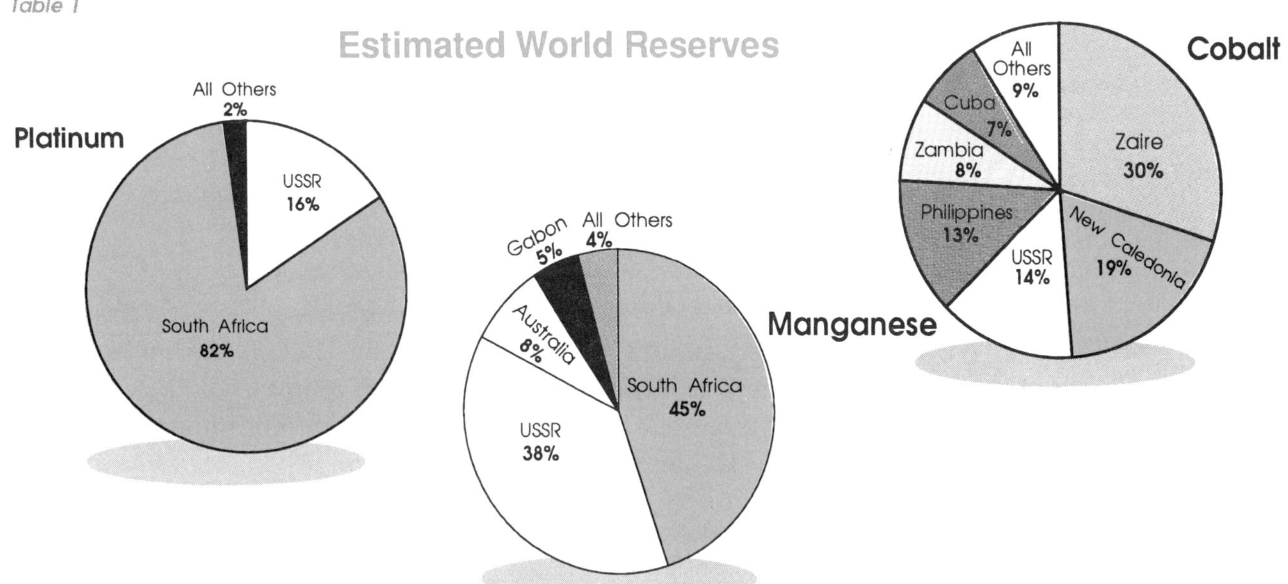

Source: *The World Almanac*, (US Interior Department, 1984)

Which crops are imported by the United States? The climate and the soil of the United States are not suitable for growing coffee plants. If it were not for trade with Colombia and Brazil, Americans would have no coffee to drink for breakfast. Bananas do not grow in the United States. Much of the fruit Americans eat in the winter comes from South America. World trade makes it possible for people in the United States to enjoy a rich and varied diet.

The United States imports many crops that cannot be grown in its climates.

What technology is imported by the United States? The United States is a leader in technology. American space flights have become everyday events. Yet some countries have products that Americans want. Many Americans prefer foreign cars, television sets and cameras to

Critical Thinking

What things would change in your life if the United States did not trade with other countries?

On Your Way Up
Organizing in a Chart
Make a chart with two columns. In the first column, list ten products that the United States imports from other countries. In the second column, list ten products that are made or grown in the United States and sold to other countries. Write a heading for each column in your chart.

American-made products. Yet, this competition is healthy because it forces the United States to make better products.

Is there another benefit of world trade? World trade has one other benefit. It keeps the United States in touch with other nations. The nations of the world need each other. Each year, the economies of all the nations in the world become more closely tied to each other. If things go badly in one nation, other nations are affected. A healthy American economy is not possible if the world economy is sick.

The nations of the world depend on each other economically.

free trade
situation in which nothing stops the flow of goods between the seller and the buyer

What is free trade? The term **free trade** means that nothing stops the flow of goods between the seller and the buyer. Some people believe that all trade should be free. If Americans want to buy Italian shoes, they should be able to. If the Russians want to buy American wheat, nothing should stop them. The people who believe in free trade would let every country do what it does best. The world would be one giant marketplace.

What are the benefits of free trade? If trade were free, all nations could use their limited resources wisely. Nations would not have to waste resources making things that other nations can make better and more cheaply. Free trade allows prices to be lower. Free trade also provides consumers with greater choices of goods to buy.

What are the dangers of free trade? Some people say that free trade is not in the best interest of the United States. They claim that American businesses need to be protected from foreign competition. For example, opponents of free trade believe that the American shoe industry might be wiped out by Italian competition. If this happened, some Americans would lose their jobs. Free trade is good economics. But politics prevents a free world market from happening.

Opponents of free trade worry about the United States being too dependent on other nations. They feel that the United States should have certain basic industries. Such industries would make the United States economically independent.

The United States depends on other countries for some of its oil supply.

Oil is the best example of the danger of free trade because oil is such a basic resource. Imagine what trouble the United States would be in if all of its oil came from the Arab states. In 1973, the Arab countries decided not to sell the United States any more oil. The reason had nothing to do with economics; it was a political decision. The decision caused serious economic problems in the United States and most of Europe. For the first time, the United States government supported research into alternate energy sources. In time, the oil began to flow again. The United States once again became dependent on foreign sources for oil. Research into other energy sources was dropped.

What is protectionism? All nations have the same concerns about too much free trade. Nations often put up trade barriers to protect home businesses and jobs. This policy is called **protectionism** (proh-TEK-shun-iz-um). There are several ways protectionism can work. The most common is the tariff, or tax on imported goods. Suppose that the United States wants to protect the American shoe industry. The government could place a high tariff on Italian shoes. This would drive up the price of Italian shoes. If the tariff is high enough, Americans will be forced to buy American-made shoes. This would save the shoe industry and its jobs. Of course, the Italians might not like this. They might raise the tariff on American imports.

protectionism
laws, quotas and tariffs to protect businesses and jobs from being hurt by foreign trade

Critical Thinking
Is protectionism good or bad? Explain.

How do quotas work? Another way protectionism works is through the **quota** (KWOHT-uh). A quota sets a limit on the number of products that can be imported. American auto makers would like to see stiff quotas placed on Japanese cars. That would limit the number of Japanese cars on the American market. With supply down, the price of Japanese cars would rise. This would make American cars seem to be a better buy.

quota
a limit set by the government on the amount of a kind of goods that can be imported

What are some other barriers to free trade? There are other ways to make it hard for importers. Red tape, or bureaucratic (byoor-oh-KRAT-ik) delays, getting through customs can greatly restrict a product's entry into the market. Sometimes, producers try to increase foreign sales by **dumping**. They price their goods lower in the foreign market than they do at home. Most nations have laws against dumping. Nations also have health and safety laws and laws concerning proper labeling. Foreign goods have to meet certain standards in order to be sold in the United States. These and other protectionist measures can hurt importers.

dumping
the practice of selling goods at a lower price in a foreign market than in the home market

Understanding What You Read

1. Why must the United States trade with other countries?
2. Name some minerals and crops that the United States imports.
3. What is free trade?
4. What are some of the benefits and dangers of free trade?
5. What is protectionism?

Workbook Activities

Chapter Test, p. 56
Reading a Chart, p. 57

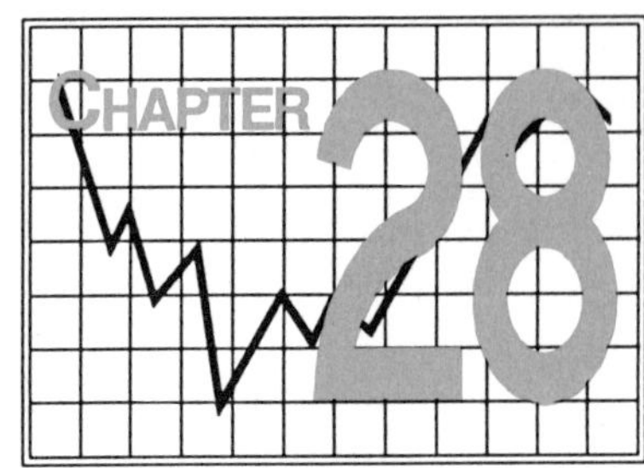

Paying for Foreign Trade

Foreign trade is necessary. But how do nations pay for it? How does the value of one nation's money compare to the value of another nation's money?

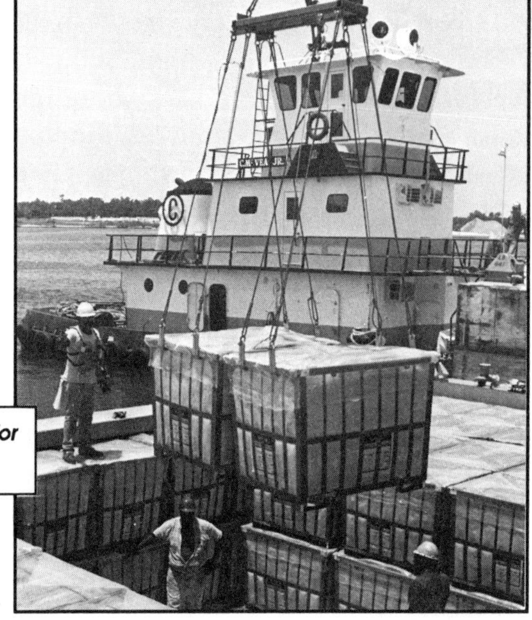

How does the United States pay for foreign trade?

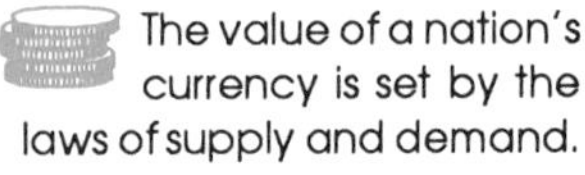

The value of a nation's currency is set by the laws of supply and demand.

How are currencies valued? Each country has its own form of currency, or money. Each one of these currencies has a different value. This value is set by the laws of supply and demand. If the demand for the Mexican peso is greater than the supply, the value of the peso goes up. If the demand for the Japanese yen is lower than the supply, the value of the yen drops. The demand for any nation's money is set by such things as inflation, the business cycle, interest rates and political stability.

exchange rate
the price of United States currency in terms of the currency of other nations

What is the exchange rate? Trade demands an exchange of one nation's money for another nation's money. Suppose you want to buy a Japanese camera. Your dollars will have to be changed into Japanese yen. The value of the dollar compared to the value of the yen is called the **exchange rate**. This rate is set by supply and demand. It changes every day and it is reported in all major urban newspapers. The daily rate change is usually small. Most nations try to keep a stable exchange rate because it makes doing business easier and more predictable. Still, the rate does change.

How to Check the Daily Foreign Exchange Rate

Suppose you want to travel to Canada or Mexico or Europe. You will need to convert your American dollars into the currency of the country you visit. Before you leave home, you can check on the exchange rate. This will serve two purposes. First, it will get you familiar with how much foreign money equals one dollar. Second, this knowledge will help to stop you from being cheated when you travel. The daily foreign exchange rate can be found in any major city newspaper. (Most smalltown newspapers do not carry the foreign exchange rate.) The exchange rate is expressed in two ways. First, it will tell you how much one peseta is worth in terms of American money. In this case, one peseta would be worth $.006, or just over one-half of one cent. Second, it will tell you how much foreign currency $1.00 will buy. In the table below, $1.00 will buy 3,122 Mexican pesos.

Foreign Exchange Rate

Monday, May 11, 1992

	$ value per unit of foreign currency		Units of currency per dollar	
	Monday	Friday	Monday	Friday
Japan (yen)	0.0007	0.00075	133.6	133.2
Germany (mark)	0.6086	0.6064	1.643	1.649
Britain (pound)	1.7857	1.7761	0.560	0.563
Canada (dollar)	0.8333	0.8382	1.200	1.193
Mexico (peso)	0.00032	0.00032	3,122	3,121

What is the balance of trade? All the nations of the world buy and sell goods and services. This can lead to three possible results. First, the amounts bought and sold can be in exact balance. When this happens, a nation's receipts (rih-SEETS), or income, equals its payments. This is called a **balance of trade** because the nation's foreign trade is said to be "in balance."

Critical Thinking
Would it be impossible to have one currency for the entire world? Why or why not?

balance of trade
a measure of the nation's imports (receipts) versus the nation's exports (payments)

What is a favorable balance? A nation rarely has its foreign trade in perfect balance. It is far more likely that the balance of trade will lean one way or the other. If receipts are larger than payments, then the nation has a surplus. This is called a favorable balance of trade. A nation with a favorable balance of trade is selling more than it is buying. There is a net flow of cash into the nation.

A nation with a favorable balance of trade is selling more products to other countries than it is buying.

Assume that a nation's receipts are smaller than its payments. When this happens, the nation has a trade deficit. This is called an unfavorable balance of trade. The nation is buying more than it is selling, and there is a net flow of cash out of the country. Figure 1 shows that, in recent years, the United States has been suffering from an unfavorable balance of trade. In fact, by the late 1980s, the United States had become the largest debtor nation in the world.

Figure 1

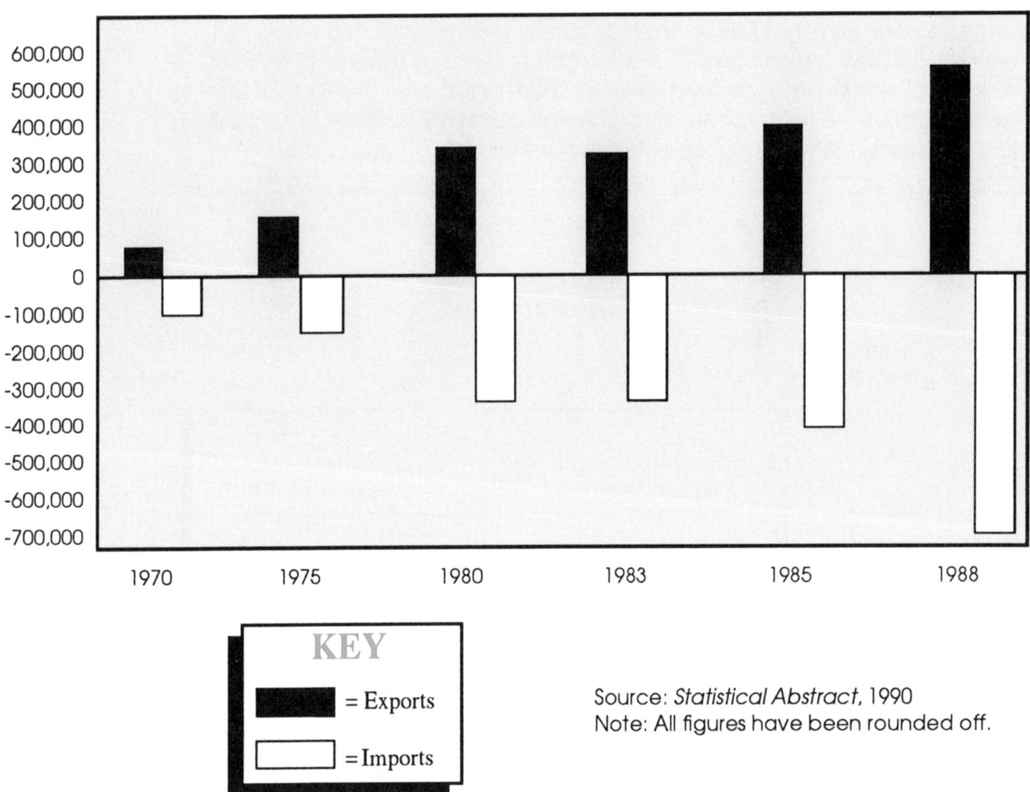

Source: *Statistical Abstract*, 1990
Note: All figures have been rounded off.

balance of payments
a detailed summary of a nation's trade with other nations

What is the balance of payments? Most nations keep a detailed summary of their trade with other nations. This summary is called the balance of payments. It includes the sale of goods and services. But it also includes such items as international loans, interest, dividends and gold reserves. The balance of payments can be divided into two main parts.

On Your Way Up
Reread
Reread the paragraphs about the current account and the capital account. Write a description of each account in your own words.

What is the current account? The current account (KUR-unt uh-KOUNT) includes the trade balance, or the difference between imported and exported goods. The current account also includes things that cannot be seen or touched, such as tourist spending, shipping costs and services. Military spending and gifts by the government to other governments are added to the current account. Since 1983, the United States has had some huge deficits in the current account.

capital account
a measurement of the movement of financial capital (money) between countries

The **capital account** (KAP-ut-ul uh-KOUNT) measures the movement of financial capital, or money, between countries. If the United States sells stocks or bonds to another country, the sale is a credit, or plus, to the capital account because the United States is gaining foreign money. On the other hand, when the United States buys stocks and bonds from another country, it is a debit, or minus, in the capital account. In recent years, the United States has borrowed far more than it has lent out. The nation has to borrow so much money because it has such large trade deficits.

Why does the United States have a debt problem? Why should a rich nation like the United States have an unfavorable balance of trade? Being rich is part of the problem. Many Americans have expensive tastes and money to spend. They celebrate with French champagne. They enjoy driving Japanese and Swedish automobiles. Many Americans like to travel overseas. Each year Americans spend billions of dollars in foreign countries.

The United States spends billions of dollars annually on foreign goods and foreign travel.

Driving a foreign car and sailing up the Nile cost money. But the effect is not the same as driving an American car and sailing down the Hudson. When Americans buy from a foreign nation, they affect the balance of payments. Their spending can cause a deficit. Suppose you pay $50 for a woolen sweater from Scotland. That money goes to Scotland. That is a minus for the balance of payments. Of course, it works the other way as well. When someone from another country visits American shores and spends money here, it is a plus for the American balance of payments.

Critical Thinking

Should foreign travel be limited when the United States has an unfavorable balance of trade? Why or why not?

On the whole, Americans have more money to spend than people in most other countries. They travel more than most other people. The United States burns more imported oil than most nations. Americans buy more imported cars, VCRs, televisions, 35mm cameras and clothing than most other people. Despite its wealth, the United States often has an unfavorable balance of trade. An unfavorable balance of trade means that other nations are holding many American dollars. This can affect the exchange rate of the dollar by making it weaker.

American consumer spending can cause a trade deficit.

Understanding What You Read

1. What is the exchange rate?
2. What is the balance of trade?
3. How can a nation have an unfavorable balance of trade?
4. What is the balance of payments?
5. What is the difference between the current account and the capital account?

Workbook Activities

Chapter Test, p. 58
Calculating the Value of the Dollar vs. Foreign Currency, p. 59

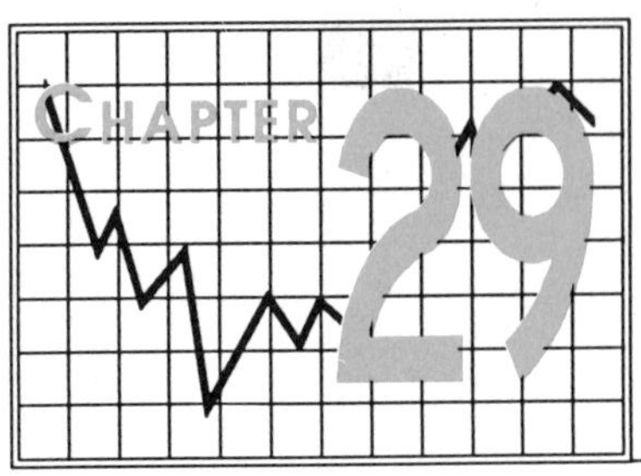

The Strength of the Dollar

When the dollar is weak, more dollars are needed to buy currency from another country.

During the 1970s, the dollar was relatively weak compared to its strength in the 1960s. When the dollar is weak, it takes more dollars to buy currency from another country. In other words, the dollar has a low exchange rate in terms of other currencies. During the early 1980s, however, the dollar had grown stronger. By 1984, some economists talked about the "unstoppable dollar." When the dollar is strong, it takes fewer dollars to buy the currency of other nations. In other words, the dollar has a high exchange rate. By 1988, the dollar had plunged once again.

Table 1 shows that in 1980 one American dollar was worth only 4.2 French francs. In 1985, that same American dollar bought 8.9 francs. Three years later, the dollar traded at 6.0 francs. In 1980, one dollar was worth about 226 Japanese yen. Five years later, the dollar bought 238 yen. In 1988, the suddenly weak dollar was worth just 128 yen. The same pattern held true for the West German mark, the British pound and the Swedish krona, as well as other major world currencies.

Table 1

FOREIGN EXCHANGE RATES, 1980 - 1990
(in units of foreign currency per dollar $)

	1980	1983	1985	1987	1988	1989	1990
Great Britain (£ - pound)	.43	.66	.76	.61	.56	.61	.56
Canada ($ - dollar)	1.17	1.23	1.36	1.32	1.23	1.18	1.16
France (ff - franc)	4.2	7.6	8.9	6.0	6.0	6.3	5.4
West Germany (m - mark)	1.8	2.5	2.8	1.7	1.7	1.8	1.6
Japan (¥ - yen)	226	237	238	144	128	138	145
Sweden (k - krona)	4.2	7.6	8.6	6.3	6.1	6.4	5.9

Source: *World Almanac*, 1992

Why did the value of the dollar change in the 1980s? Most economists point to the high interest rates of the early 1980s as the reason for the sudden surge in the strength of the dollar. These high rates were caused by the huge budget deficits. The government had to borrow billions. This drove up the interest rates. But even when interest rates came down, the dollar stayed strong. This showed that the world had great confidence in the American economy. It was growing faster than the economies of most other nations.

High interest rates can increase the strength of the dollar.

The dollar plunged during the late 1980s because the United States began to run up huge trade deficits. Americans bought large amounts of foreign goods and services during this time. All this foreign buying increased the demand for foreign currencies. At the same time, other nations were not buying similar amounts from the United States. This decreased the demand for the American dollar and lowered its value on the world's money markets.

Large trade deficits can weaken the dollar.

A strong dollar sounds like a good thing, but nothing in economics is ever that simple. The strong dollar of the mid-1980s was a mixed blessing, and so was the weak dollar of the late 1980s.

Why is a weak dollar both good and bad? Two bad things happen when the dollar is relatively weak. First, imports decrease. This hurts the consumer because foreign goods become much more costly. Second, travel to foreign countries costs Americans more.

A weak dollar makes buying foreign goods more expensive for Americans.

A weak dollar cuts the sale of imported products, such as Mexican pottery, German cameras and Japanese cars. They all become very high in price. This forces most consumers to "buy American." This is good for the American business because foreign competition is priced out of the market. But shouldn't Americans be able to buy foreign goods as well as American goods?

The other bad news is for American tourists. When you visit Canada, you change your dollars into Canadian dollars. The number of Canadian dollars you receive in return depends on the strength of the American dollar in terms of the Canadian dollar. If the American dollar is weak, you will get fewer Canadian dollars in return. This means that your vacation will be more costly.

A weak dollar makes foreign travel more expensive for Americans.

On the other hand, a weak dollar does some good things. Figure 1 shows that a weak dollar increases exports. Americans can more easily sell their goods in foreign countries. If the dollar is weak, American cars are cheaper for European consumers. If more cars are sold, there may be more jobs for the Americans who make them. A weak dollar also brings more

A weak dollar increases exports.

Critical Thinking
Why is the strength of the dollar of such concern to the world?

foreign tourists to the United States. When the dollar is weak, an American vacation is a bargain for people from other countries. The yen, the pound, the mark and the franc go further when they are converted into less expensive dollars.

Figure 1

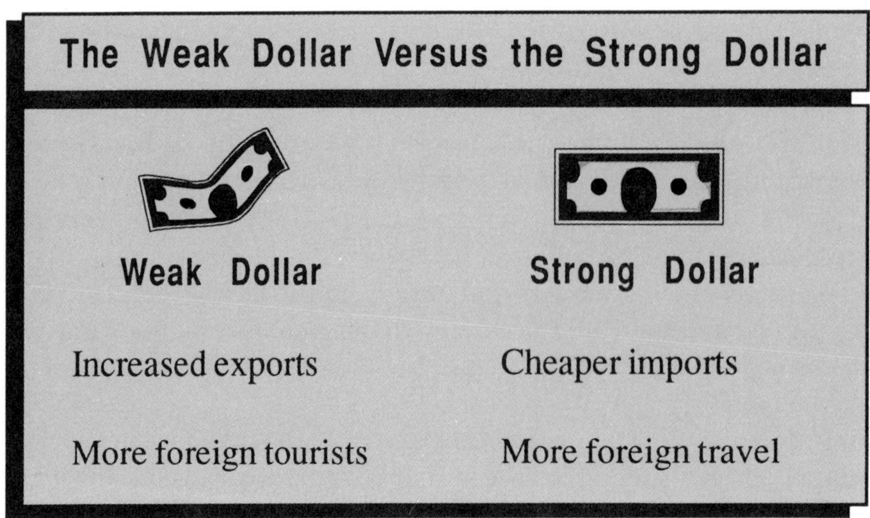

The Weak Dollar Versus the Strong Dollar
Weak Dollar
Strong Dollar
Increased exports
Cheaper imports
More foreign tourists
More foreign travel

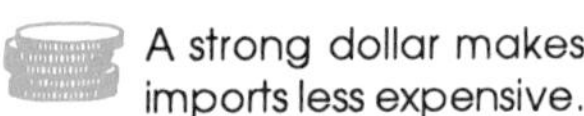
A strong dollar makes imports less expensive.

Why is a strong dollar both bad and good? When the dollar is strong, the situation is reversed. Figure 1 shows that a strong dollar makes imports seem cheap. French wine becomes a bargain, and the sticker price of foreign cars falls. The strong dollar is also great news for the American tourist. In 1985, the dollar went almost twice as far in Great Britain as it did in 1980. This made foreign travel possible for more Americans. The strong dollar also made the price of imported oil cheaper. This helped to lower gas prices. Because imports were so cheap, American businesses could keep their prices low. This has helped to keep inflation under control.

Travel by foreigners to the United States is reduced by a strong dollar. A trip to New York or the Rocky Mountains costs foreigners more when the dollar is stronger. Americans in the tourist business lose foreign customers when the dollar is strong.

A strong dollar decreases exports.

Critical Thinking
Which Americans are hurt by a strong dollar? Why?

What does a strong dollar mean to exporters? A strong dollar hurts American exporters. Figure 2 shows that American goods can have a hard time competing overseas when the dollar is strong. Few Germans or Italians could afford to buy an American car. The strong dollar of the mid-1980s doubled the cost of American cars in the European market in just a few years. The story was the same with other American products. They were just too costly for foreigners to buy. Even the American farmer was being undersold.

Figure 2

Trade Imbalance

(in billions of dollars)

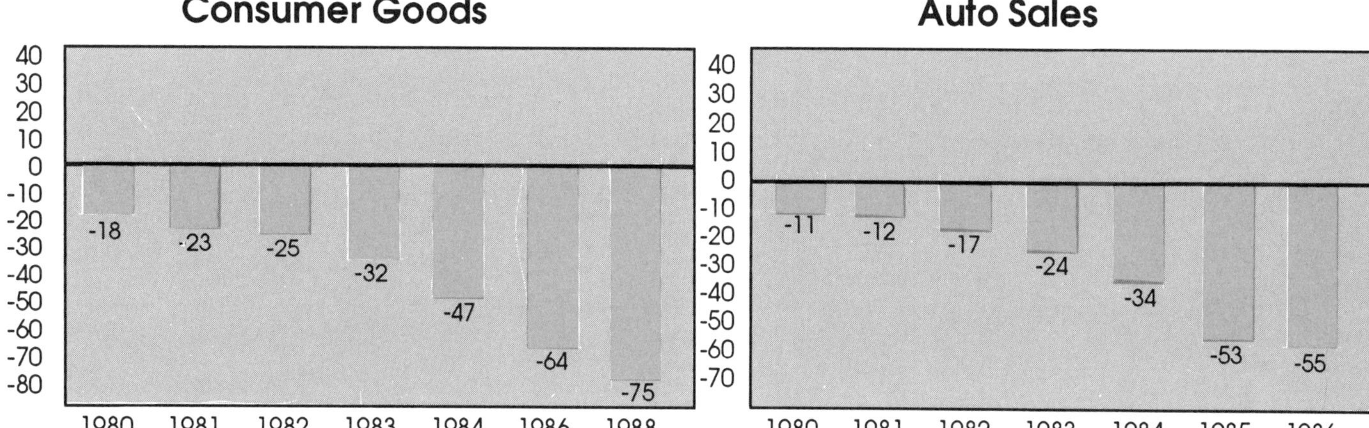

Source: *Statistical Abstract*, 1990

A strong dollar can mean lost jobs. These jobs are lost in industries based on exports. Whether or not enough new jobs are created by increased imports is an open question. In any event, the strong dollar does create hardships for some workers. It can also cause trouble for America's trading partners. When a strong dollar makes American goods costly, the rate of inflation goes up in countries that buy American products.

> **On Your Way Up**
> **Review**
> Write a summary about the advantages and disadvantages of both a strong and a weak dollar. Write the summary in your own words so you will remember.

Understanding What You Read

1. What makes the dollar strong or weak?
2. What are the bad effects of a weak dollar?
3. How does a weak dollar affect American business?
4. What are the bad effects of a strong dollar?
5. What are the good effects of a strong dollar?

Workbook Activities

Chapter Test, p. 60
Calculating the Strength of the Dollar, p. 61

Final Test, pp. 62-63

Empower Yourself - Cooperative Learning

Look at the chart that your group made to compare American-made and imported products. Add up the prices of all the American-made products that the group would have bought instead of the imported item. Do the same for all the imported items that you preferred.

Compare the amount you would have spent on American-made goods with the amount you would have spent on imported goods. How would your spending have affected the balance of trade?

Review

On a separate sheet of paper, write the numbers from 1 to 16. Next to each number, write the word or word phrase in parentheses that makes each sentence correct.

1. The United States is so rich that it (does / does not) need the goods and services other countries can provide.
2. In free trade, (nothing / protectionism) stops the flow of goods between the seller and the buyer.
3. Tariffs that keep businesses from being hurt by foreign trade are a form of (protectionism / quotas).
4. (A quota / Dumping) is a limit set by the government on the amount of different kinds of goods that can be imported.
5. Nations often put up (trade barriers / protectionism).
6. The (exchange rate / balance of trade) is the price of United States currency in terms of the currency of other nations.
7. American consumer spending (does / does not) affect the trade deficit.
8. The value of a nation's currency is set by (its government / the law of supply and demand).
9. A measure of the nation's imports versus the nation's exports is the (balance of trade / receipts).
10. When a nation's exports are greater than its imports, it has a(n) (favorable / unfavorable) balance of trade.
11. The (balance of payments / balance of trade) is a detailed summary of a nation's trade with other nations.
12. The difference between the costs of imported and exported goods is the (trade balance / deficit).
13. The measurement of the movement of money between countries is the (current / capital) account.
14. When the dollar is weak, it takes (fewer / more) dollars to buy currency.
15. A strong dollar makes imports (more / less) expensive.
16. Large trade deficits (strengthen / weaken) the dollar.

Glossary

A

ability-to-pay tax: A tax in which those who earn the most money pay the most taxes. The progressive tax is an ability-to-pay tax.

acid rain: Smoke pollution that falls in the form of rain and destroys our lakes, rivers, trees, and wildlife.

advertisement: A company's notice of prices, and often its sales, to get people to buy its product.

assessor: A person who estimates the value of property for tax purposes.

B

balance of payments: A detailed summary of a nation's trade with other nations.

balance of trade: A measure of the nation's imports (payments) versus the nation's exports (receipts). When imports are greater than exports, we have an unfavorable balance of trade. When imports are less than exports, we have a favorable balance of trade.

balanced budget: A budget in which income and spending are equal.

barter: To exchange one thing of value for something else of value.

benefits-received tax: A tax in which those who get the service pay the tax.

boycott: A refusal to buy a company's products. A boycott is used to force a company to change some condition.

business cycle: The ups and downs of the economy.

C

capital: One of the factors of production. It is money and goods from which income is earned.

capital account: A measurement of the movement of financial capital (money) between countries.

capitalism: An economic system based on private ownership of property. The government plays a limited role in the economy. The driving force behind capitalism is the profit motive plus competition.

closed shop: The hiring by employers of union members only.

collectives: Large farms created from small, private farms that had been seized by the government and joined together.

collective bargaining: A meeting of union leaders and employers to work out an agreement on wages and fringe benefits.

command economy: An economic system under which all the decisions are made by a central power. Communism is an example of a command economy.

commercial bank: A bank that offers all banking services to consumers.

commission: An economic system under which all the factors of production are owned by the state and shared by the people as a whole.

competition: The contest between two or more sellers to attract buyers.

compound interest: Interest paid on money you have in the bank and on the interest that money has earned.

constant dollars: A way to measure the GNP allowing for inflation.

consumer: Any person who buys or uses a good or service.

consumer goods: Products made for use by people.

consumer spending: The flow of income in an economy that results when businesses pay workers and workers spend their income, creating profits for business and continuing the cycle.

contraction: The final phase of the business cycle when consumer demand falls and unemployment rises.

corporate income tax: A tax placed on business.

corporation: A form of business organization. It acts as a "legal" person. It can buy and sell. It can sue or be sued. The corporation is owned by people who hold its stocks.

cost-push inflation: An increase in the level of prices caused by increased production costs.

credit: The buying of goods and services with the promise to pay later.

currency: A term used to describe paper money and coins.

current dollars: A way to measure the GNP without allowing for inflation.

D

deduction: Money taken from your gross pay for such things as taxes, insurance and pension plans.

deficit spending: The act of spending the money the government knows it does not have.

deflation: A general drop in the level of prices.

demand: The amount of a good or service that consumers are willing to buy at all possible prices at a given time.

demand deposits: Money kept in a checking account. People can "demand" their money in their accounts by writing checks.

demand-pull inflation: An increase in the level of prices caused by increased demand for the good or service.

democracy: A political system in which the people enjoy freedom and elect their own leaders.

depression: A period of very high unemployment and low economic activity. It usually occurs over a fairly long period of time.

dictatorship: A political system in which the government tells people how to live. There is little freedom.

discount rate: The interest rate the Federal Reserve charges its member banks.

disposable personal income: The total amount of money people have left over after paying all their direct personal taxes.

dividend: A payment to a stockholder by a corporation, or to a depositor in a mutual savings bank.

division of labor: Different people doing different parts of a job to make a product, rather than one person making one product.

dumping: The practice of selling goods at a lower price in a foreign market than in the home market.

durable goods: Goods that last a long time and can be used over and over again, such as cars and houses.

E

economics: A science that studies how and why goods and services are produced and used.

elastic demand: A demand that varies with price. When price goes up, demand goes down.

excess profits: The money earned over and above normal profits.

exchange rate: The price of United States currency in terms of the currency of other nations.

excise tax: A tax on an item such as tobacco.

expansion: The part of the business cycle when supply, demand, and employment are high.

exports: Goods sold by American businesses to other nations.

F

factors of production: Land, labor, capital and management. They are combined to produce goods and services.

Federal Reserve System: The central bank of the United States, which is run by a Board of Governors.

fiscal policy: The taxing and spending policies of the government.

fixed interest rate: The interest rate on a mortgage that stays the same, even with changing prices due to inflation.

flexible interest rate: The interest rate on a mortgage that changes with inflation.

free enterprise: The freedom of any person to enter into any legal business he or she wants to enter.

free market: In a market system, where the buying and selling take place. p. 3

fringe benefits: Non-cash payments to workers. These can include vacation time, health plans, and pension programs.

G

Gosplan: The central power in the former Soviet Union that made all economic decisions.

Gross National Product (GNP): The total value, in current dollars, of all goods and services produced in the United States for a given year.

gross pay: The total amount of money a worker makes before deductions.

I

imports: Goods sold in the United States from other nations.

income: The money a person earns.

incorporated (Inc.): The forming of a corporation.

inelastic demand: Demand that does not change with price. When price goes up, demand stays the same.

inflation: A general rise in the level of prices.

injunction: A court order to stop something from happening.

interest: The price paid for the use of money.

intermediate goods: Goods used to make other goods.

investment: The purchase of goods and services or land in the hope that its value will increase with time.

"invisible hand": The market force Adam Smith said creates fair prices, good products and a fair wage.

L

labor union: An organization of workers to promote the interests of its members.

loose money: Sometimes called "easy money." It is a term used to describe low interest rates.

luxuries: Goods and services that are not necessary.

M

macroeconomics: The study of an economy as a whole.

management: Another one of the factors of production. It is the human element which combines land, labor and capital to produce goods and services.

market economy: An economic system based on the working of the marketplace; an economy governed by the laws of supply and demand.

medium of exchange: Money or something else that buys goods and services.

microeconomics: The study of the economy's small details.

mixed economy: A capitalist economy in which the government plays a limited role.

monetary policy: How the Federal Reserve System affects the supply of money and the interest rates we pay for loans.

money: Anything that people will accept as payment.

monopoly: The complete control of the market by one seller.

mortgage: A long-term loan to buy a house or other high-priced property.

motivation: An extra benefit such as money that gets someone to do something.

multiplier effect: An economic rule that states that one extra dollar in the economy will produce five extra dollars worth of spending.

N

national debt: The amount of money the national government owes.

national income: The total value of goods and services produced by the nation for a year.

nationalization: The taking over of private industry by the government.

necessities: Goods and services that people must have, such as food.

net national product: The GNP minus worn-out plants and equipment.

net pay: The amount of money received in a paycheck after deductions.

nondurable goods: Goods that don't last long, such as food and gas.

normal profits: The lowest profits that will keep a business going.

O

open-market operations: The buying and selling of government securities by the Federal Reserve.

opportunity costs: The price we pay for using our limited resources one way and not another.

overproduction: Making too much of a product, as often happens in farming.

overtime pay: Pay for work done above 40 hours.

P

peak: The part of the business cycle when there is usually the highest inflation. Production, demand and employment are also at their highest.

per capita: The measure of anything for one person.

personal income: The total amount of money people earn or are given by the government.

personal income tax: A tax paid on all wages, salaries and other forms of income paid to the individual.

piecework: A wage based on the number of pieces produced.

pollution: Dirt that hurts the water, air, or other natural resources.

poverty line: The lowest amount of money a family of four needs to live.

price-wage spiral: A cycle where prices go up, then wages go up, then prices, then wages, and so on.

producer goods: Products used to make consumer goods or services.

productivity: A measure of how effectively workers work.

profit: Money made from a business.

profit motive: The desire of sellers to make money.

profit-sharing: A plan where an employer gives the workers a part of the profits of the company.

progressive tax: A tax system which takes a higher percentage from the rich than from the poor.

property tax: A tax charged to owners of property based on its value.

proportional tax: A tax system in which all people pay the same percentage.

protectionism: laws, quotas, and tariffs to protect businesses and jobs from being hurt by free trade.

public utility: Gas and electric, water, bus and other services owned by everyone, not by a private company.

pure competition: A large number of sellers with the same product, such as farming, selling to a large number of buyers. With so much competition, the sellers cannot control price or supply.

Q

quota: A limit set by the government on the amount of goods that can be imported.

R

rate of inflation: A percentage that shows how fast the dollar is losing value.

Reaganomics: A policy of cutting taxes and government spending.

real goods: Goods produced by businesses using the factors of production.

real wages: What your money will actually buy.

receipts: A nations' income.

recession: A moderate slowdown in the economy, and profits and prices fall. Due to the slowdown, a number of people are without jobs.

regular wages: Pay for a week's work of 35-40 hours.

reserve requirement: The percentage of a bank's deposits that must be held by the bank or in the Federal Reserve vaults.

resources: The supply of things that people have to fill their needs.

S

salary: Fixed pay for regular work, such as what teachers receive.

scarcity: A condition of limited resources. Scarcity occurs because wants are larger than resources. People cannot have everything they want. They must make choices.

securities: Proofs of ownership. The government buys and sells securities to raise or lower the money supply.

Social Security tax: A payroll tax taken from your paycheck and paid to retired workers.

socialism: An economic system in which the means of production are owned by the public. People may run small businesses, and they can own goods for personal use.

stagflation: A period of high inflation and slow economic growth.

stock: A piece of a corporation owned by an individual.

stock market: A place where stocks are bought and sold.

strike: A work stoppage to put pressure on the employer to meet certain demands.

supply: The amount of goods and services producers are willing to supply at all possible prices at a given time.

supply-side economics: A system of increased supply. Supply-siders think demand will take care of itself. They do not like price and wage controls.

surplus: The amount over and above what is needed.

T

tariff: A tax on imported goods.

technology: The use of science to produce goods and services.

tight money: A term used to describe high interest rates. It is often used to describe the policy of the Federal Reserve System when it raises interest rates.

trade-off: The act of choosing which things you want most.

traditional economy: An economic system in which decisions are made by customs and old beliefs.

transfer payments: Tax money taken from the rich and given to the poor.

trough: The part of the business cycle when there is a depression. Demand and production are very low and unemployment is high.

U

unemployment compensation: Income paid by the government to people who have been laid off from their jobs.

union shop: When an employer hires someone on the condition that the person joins the union. There are right-to -work laws against this.

W

wages-in-kind: Non-cash pay, such as room and board.

wealth: The value of what a person owns.

Index